ELIZABETH CADY STANTON

Erratum: pp. 94-95
should be reversed.

Elizabeth Cady Stanton and two of her sons. From a daguerrotype, 1848.

ELIZABETH CADY STANTON

Mary Ann B. Oakley

B
Stanton

ISBN: 0-912670-03-7

Library of Congress Catalog Card Number: 72 80249

Manufactured in the United States of America. Composed by O.B.U., New York, N.Y.
Printed by the Faculty Press, Brooklyn, N.Y. 159

To Godfrey, with love

CONTENTS

ELIZABETH CADY STANTON

PROLOGUE

Since nobody seemed to have a key to the Wesleyan Chapel in Seneca Falls, New York, a man climbed in through the window and unlocked the door. The small crowd which had gathered outside filed into the church, buzzing with curious chatter. No one had been to a meeting like this before. Most people present had read the newspaper announcement calling for a discussion of the "social, civil, and religious condition and rights of women." But what was this "convention" to accomplish?

The first day's session had been planned for women only, but so many interested men had come that the women agreed to let them stay. Since none of those who had issued the call to the convention felt experienced enough to conduct a public meeting, they asked James Mott, a tall, stately Quaker, to take the chair. His wife, Lucretia Mott, who was accustomed to speaking at Quaker meetings, stated the purpose of the gathering and urged all the women present to speak out.

Then Elizabeth Cady Stanton arose and read the Declaration of Sentiments which the organizing committee had prepared:

> We hold these truths to be self-evident, that all men and women are created equal; that they are endowed by their

11

> Creator with certain inalienable rights; that among these are
> life, liberty, and the pursuit of happiness. . . . The history of
> mankind is a history of repeated injuries and usurpations on
> the part of man toward woman, having in direct object the
> establishment of an absolute tyranny over her. To prove this,
> let facts be submitted to a candid world. . . .

She listed such grievances as these: married women were
dead under the law, with no rights to property or even
to their own children; women could not vote; even
those single women who owned property were taxed
without representation; women had no opportunity for
education or decent jobs.[1]

The remainder of the day was spent discussing the
Declaration, and it was unanimously adopted the following morning. Then various resolutions were presented and discussed one by one. Woman was created
the equal of man and should be so recognized. Woman
should be allowed to assume whatever social or public
position she wished, insofar as her capabilities allowed
her. The group voted unanimously for the adoption of
one after another of these resolutions, as radical as they
were.

Then the same young woman from Seneca Falls who
had read the Declaration of Sentiments rose again. In a
clear, firm tone, she presented the particular resolution
that she had prepared:

> Resolved, that it is the duty of the women of this country to
> secure to themselves their sacred right to the elective fran-
> chise.[2]

A great murmuring filled the room as people turned to
their neighbors to declare their shock or admiration.

12

"Is this possible? And right here in public," remarked a man.

"How bold! Where did she ever get the nerve to say such a thing?" several of the women asked.

Elizabeth Cady Stanton had dared to suggest that women be permitted to *vote*!

It was July 1848. A revolution was under way.

CHAPTER ONE

The large house was chilly that morning as the Scottish nurse led the four-year-old into a cheerful, white-curtained room. Elizabeth was pleased to meet her new sister though she could not understand why so many people were saying, "What a pity she's a girl!" Since the Cady family now had five daughters and one son, it was naturally of some concern that there was only one male heir. But Elizabeth was not yet old enough to understand the source of that concern or even to know that girls were considered inferior to boys.[3]

Before many years had passed, Elizabeth Cady was to encounter the "defect of sex" much more sharply. Until then, she grew up in the usual manner of a daughter in an upper-class American family. She had been born in Johnstown, New York, November 12, 1815, the year that her father, Judge Daniel Cady, was elected to Congress. Her mother, Margaret Livingston Cady, was a tall, regal woman whom Elizabeth admired for her courage and ability to seem at ease in any situation. With six children, a staff of servants, and an active household to manage, Margaret Cady was always busy.

Young Elizabeth was much more deeply influenced by her father, whom she feared and whom she strove to please—often in vain—until his death. She later wrote that her father was at ease only at his own fireside and in the courthouse. He was well known for his integrity and sensitivity; everyone respected him. The Cady children feared, rather than loved, their parents, who were kind and somewhat indulgent but limited by the strict Puritan ethic so common in that day.

The young Cadys were supervised by a series of Scottish nurses, whom they disliked intensely. Their nurses, in turn, considered them stubborn and disobedient children. Elizabeth was often punished for what she later called "justifiable acts of rebellion against the tyranny of those in authority." She and her younger sister Margaret took special pleasure in defying the strict rules that governed their young lives. These fun-loving, high-spirited girls learned to question anything which restricted their freedom to grow and develop.

The Cady children were especially fond of three black servants who watched after them and often rescued them from the unfortunate effects of some prank. Unlike the children's parents or nurses, these men seemed neither stern nor forbidding. Abraham, Peter, and Jacob took some of the children with them as they went about their errands around Johnstown. The children often attended services with Peter at the Episcopal Church and sat with him in the "Negro pew." Once, when Peter went to take communion alone, after all of the white church members had returned from the altar, one of the young Cadys followed him down the aisle and knelt beside him, innocently mocking the prejudices of the congregation. Peter took Elizabeth with him on his errands or visits to the jail, the courthouse, and her father's law office. She preferred these places to other attractions in Johnstown.

When Elizabeth Cady was eleven, her older brother,

16

Eleazer, who had just completed his course of studies at Union College, died as the result of an accident. Eleazer had been his father's special joy, and Judge Cady was overcome with grief at his loss.

Elizabeth tried to comfort her father. "We all miss him so deeply," she said. "But you know we love you, too, and we will strive all the more to be the kind of children you would like us to be."

"Oh, my daughter," sighed Judge Cady, "I wish you were a boy!"[4]

Somewhat puzzled, Elizabeth thought about the matter. As she lay in bed that night, she decided that she would take her brother's place. "Father will be so pleased," she thought. "I will study Greek and learn to ride a horse. That's what boys always do. Oh, Father will be so pleased with me!"

Early the next morning Elizabeth went to her neighbor and pastor, the Reverend Simon Hosack, as he was working in his garden. "My father," she told him sadly, "prefers boys to girls. So I intend to be as near like one as possible. I am going to ride horseback and study Greek. Will you help me?" Elizabeth was a special favorite of the old pastor, and he immediately provided the first Greek lesson.

For several months Elizabeth accompanied her father to her brother's grave while he mourned his loss. Very little was said during these sad outings. Elizabeth continued to study diligently, always intent on one goal: to please her father and compensate for the loss of his son. Her teacher was amazed at her rapid progress. Then came the moment when she was ready to show her father how well she was doing. The Reverend Mr. Hosack looked on proudly. But Judge Cady only sighed, "Oh, you should have been a boy!" Elizabeth was so

17

disappointed that even her beloved teacher could not console her; she determined to study even harder.

She attended the Johnstown Academy where she studied Greek, Latin, and mathematics with a class of boys. All year long she set her sights on the second prize in Greek. "If I win that," she thought, "Father cannot help but be pleased." Finally the day arrived when her efforts were rewarded with the Greek Testament. She ran all the way home to show her prize to Judge Cady and eagerly awaited his praise. Her father was indeed proud of her, but once more she heard the bitter phrase, "My daughter, it's a pity you were not a boy."

In tears, Elizabeth ran to the Reverend Mr. Hosack. Trying to comfort her, he said, "My child, I am so proud of you and what you have done that I am going to will you my Greek lexicon, my Testament and grammar, and my four volumes of Scott's commentaries." Elizabeth was grateful for his kindness and confidence in her. She greatly appreciated his encouragement, but she began to wonder why boys were so important. Why were daughters considered inferior to sons? Why did her accomplishments mean less to her father merely because of her sex?

At this time Elizabeth began spending many of her free hours in her father's law office. She listened to his clients, talked with the students who were reading law with him, and read some of the laws about women. She learned that a father usually willed his property to his eldest son, upon whom the mother then became financially dependent. If the relationship between the mother and son (or daughter-in-law) were not smooth, the result could be tragic for the older woman. Elizabeth soon began to understand the cruelty and injustice experienced by married women with no rights

18

to property or even to the little money they might earn. She saw women who sewed all day or raised a few chickens to make some cash for badly-needed food; their husbands might then take the money and buy whiskey or gamble while their children went hungry.

Judge Cady and his students showed Elizabeth some of these unjust laws in the law books that lined the office shelves. "I am going to take my scissors and cut those laws out of the books just as soon as I have the opportunity," she resolved to herself. When she confided her plan to Flora Campbell, one of her father's clients, Flora told Judge Cady. Without letting Elizabeth know that he was aware of her intentions, the Judge explained to her that his law books were but one set of many, that removing pages from the books would not change the laws at all. "When you are older," he told her, "you must go to Albany and tell the legislators how those laws wrong women." Elizabeth was challenged, and she never forgot. She determined that somehow she would change those unjust statutes.

As Elizabeth Cady continued her studies at the Johnstown Academy, she worked and played freely with the boys there. She had long assumed that, like her male classmates, she would attend Union College after completing the course at the Academy. When she learned that Union College did not admit female students, she was appalled. "It is humiliating that such a distinction should be made merely on grounds of sex," she protested, but there was nothing she could do.

After that, she busied herself for a time riding, playing chess, and arguing with her father's law students about woman's rights. "It seemed to me," she later wrote, "that every book taught the 'divinely ordained' headship of man; but my mind never yielded to this

19

popular heresy."

Finally Elizabeth entered Emma Willard's Female Seminary at Troy, New York. She did not look forward to school without the stimulation of boys, and she had already studied everything taught there except dancing, music, and French. Her experiences at the seminary convinced her that coeducation was very important to healthy moral and intellectual development. She strongly disliked the jealousies, gossip, and friction she encountered among the girls in the school; she found them not accustomed to serious thinking.

When she had been at Emma Willard's only a brief time, she heard one of her friends call, "Heads out!"

"What is it?" cried Elizabeth, expecting to see some wild animal or freak.

"Why, don't you see those boys?" asked a classmate.

"Oh," replied a disappointed Elizabeth. "Is that all? I have seen boys all my life." Boys to her were friends and classmates, not something special for girls to giggle about.

The most important event during Elizabeth's stay at Mrs. Willard's was her unfortunate exposure to the Reverend Dr. Charles G. Finney, ex-president of Oberlin College and one of the most famous evangelists of the era. The Cady family belonged to the Scotch Presbyterian Church, and Elizabeth had been reared in a strong and gloomy Calvinist tradition. As the Cady children had found fear of their parents a stronger emotion than love, so fear predominated in their conceptions of God. Even as a child Elizabeth had questioned her nurse, "Why is everything I like a sin and everything I dislike commanded by God? I am so tired of that everlasting no! no! no! I suppose God will say 'no' to all we like in the next world." Eventually all the negativism of her

20

Calvinistic upbringing came to focus in the ringing of church bells, which filled her with dread and fear. She was unhappy when she thought about hell and the devil—always presented vividly to scare young children into virtuous behavior.

When Elizabeth, along with her classmates, attended Dr. Finney's public services and the daily prayer meetings at the seminary, she became one of his "first victims." She later described how even the most innocent girl felt like an evil monster and was sure she was eternally damned. She went to Dr. Finney in her unhappiness. "I cannot understand what I am to do. If you should tell me to go to the top of the church steeple and jump off, I would readily do it, if thereby I could save my soul; but I do not know how to go to Jesus."

Said Dr. Finney, "Repent and believe, that is all you have to do to be happy here and hereafter."

"I am very sorry," replied a distressed Elizabeth, "for all the evil I have done, and I believe all you tell me, and the more sincerely I believe, the more unhappy I am."

Elizabeth felt that Dr. Finney actually harmed the very persons he sought to save. She had nightmares about lost and damned souls. Her fear and anguish grew until she nearly suffered an emotional collapse. After she returned to Johnstown, she frequently awoke her father in the middle of the night. "Pray for me," she begged him. "I fear that I will be cast into hell before morning."

The family decided to send Elizabeth to Niagara with her father, her sister, and her brother-in-law. For six weeks the entire subject of religion was a forbidden topic of conversation. Elizabeth discussed liberal and rational ideas with her brother-in-law; she read Combe's

Constitution of Man and *Moral Philosophy*. Eventually her sunny disposition returned and her religious anxiety disappeared. From the experience she gained a conviction that children should never be exposed to gloomy ideas and fears.

The years following those at Mrs. Willard's were among the most pleasant of Elizabeth's girlhood. Friends and relatives were always in and out of the Cady house, and there were frequent visits to neighboring towns and cities. Her brother-in-law, Edward Bayard, ten years her senior, led the young people in discussions of law, history, poetry, novels, politics, economics, and philosophy. They read Scott, Bulwer, James, Cooper, and Dickens. Such intellectual stimulation alternated pleasantly with music, dancing, games, riding, and walking. Less enjoyable were the chores: mending, sewing, ironing.

Edward Bayard, husband of Elizabeth's oldest sister, Tryphena, was a constant influence on and protector of the younger Cady girls. Life dulled in Johnstown after Edward and Tryphena moved to Seneca Falls, New York, where Edward opened a law office. When Elizabeth visited them, she enjoyed the long conversations with Edward. In the midst of one of these, he suddenly broke down and confessed that he loved her.[5] Elizabeth, shaken, knew that she shared Edward's feelings, and she longed to tell him so. But loyalty to her sister kept her silent.

Edward threw himself into his new interest, homeopathic medicine. And he continued to love Elizabeth all his life. The experience was especially difficult for her because she could confide in no one. Her loyalty to Tryphena was too intense for her to reveal her problem. There were brief flirtations with other young men. "The problem with me," Elizabeth said to one of her friends, "is that I have been around boys too much to idealize the sex."

One haven for Elizabeth during the late 1830s was the home of Cousin Gerrit Smith at Peterboro, New York. Gerrit Smith was a reformer, an abolitionist, and a friend to all who knew him. His comfortable home was a station on the underground railroad; many escaping slaves were grateful for his hospitality as they fled to Canada. Gerrit and Nancy Smith had rejected the strict Calvinism in which they were reared because of the church's ambiguous attitude toward slavery. They advocated and practiced a practical Christianity in daily life rather than espousing any formal creed. At Peterboro Elizabeth realized for the first time that religion could be a source of comfort as well as of fear.

At Peterboro Elizabeth also became involved in antislavery discussions after having heard speeches by such outstanding leaders of the abolitionist movement as William Lloyd Garrison and Wendell Phillips. The movement had been growing in activity and size since 1831 when Garrison published the first edition of his newspaper, *The Liberator*. During these eight years, too, differences developed within the movement, especially around the question of immediate emancipation. Radicals like Garrison, like the august orator Phillips, and the former slave, Frederick Douglass, believed in uncompromising, immediate emancipation. They distrusted voting as a tool for change. Gradualists like Gerritt Smith believed in reform through the ballot. Many gradualists, however, were not averse to using such illegal methods as the underground railroad.

One day, as Elizabeth and other women were singing in the parlor, Cousin Gerrit appeared and said mysteriously, "I have a most important secret to tell you, which you must keep to yourselves religiously for twenty-four hours."

Solemnly, the women promised. "Now," he said, "follow me to the third story."

The women looked at one another with curious expressions. At last Cousin Gerrit opened a door. Entering a large room, they saw a light-skinned black woman, about eighteen years old. Cousin Gerrit spoke to her, "Harriet, I have brought all my young cousins to see you. I want you to make good abolitionists of them by telling them the history of your life—what you have seen and suffered in slavery."

He turned to the others. "Harriet has just escaped from her master, who is visiting in Syracuse, and she is on her way to Canada. She will start this evening and you may never have another opportunity of seeing a slave girl face to face, so ask her all you care to know of the system of slavery."

For two hours Harriet told them about her life, how, when she was only fourteen, she had been taken from her family and sold for her beauty in a slave market in New Orleans. As she talked, the others wept openly. By the time Cousin Gerrit returned, they needed no further urging to become abolitionists.

Harriet, dressed as a Quaker, left at twilight for Oswego and the lake-crossing to Canada. The very next day her master and the marshal from Syracuse appeared at Gerrit Smith's door. He graciously received them and invited them to search the house and grounds if they so desired. Then he asked them to stay for dinner, detaining them as long as possible to give Harriet every extra minute to escape. Harriet's former master was surprised to find an abolitionist so courteous and pleasant. Before the visitors left, they shook hands with Gerrit and said they hoped some solution to the problem of slavery could be found. Elizabeth and her friends cried with joy when word came that Harriet was indeed safe in Canada.

One of the many visitors to Peterboro was an eloquent young orator for the abolitionist cause, Henry Brewster Stanton. He arrived late in 1839 from Utica, New York, with a young woman to whom, it was rumored, he was engaged. Elizabeth and her friends, believing that Stanton was not a matrimonial prospect, felt much freer to be themselves than they would have otherwise. Elizabeth, who disliked coy flirtations anyhow, was deeply impressed when she heard Henry Stanton speak at Madison County antislavery meetings. "He is not so smooth and eloquent as Wendell Phillips," she mused, "but he can make his audience laugh and cry. Even Phillips admits he cannot move his audience to tears."

Henry Stanton was as good a conversationalist as he was a public speaker. Each morning two carriage-loads of people left to attend one of the meetings, often as far as ten miles away. Through the hills of Madison County in the crisp autumn air they drove, returning frequently by moonlight. Elizabeth was as happy as she had ever been in her life. She was inspired by new ideas of the rights of the individual and the basic principles of American government, by the discussions of temperance, and by arguments over abolitionist strategy. Henry Stanton, like Gerrit Smith and most of the New York abolitionists, believed in gradual reform within the system. They refused to go along with William Lloyd Garrison's "No Union with Slaveholders" movement. Garrison wanted to eliminate slave states from the Union, and even went so far as to call the Constitution "a covenant with death and an agreement with hell." Stanton and Smith urged every abolitionist to vote for candidates who opposed the extension of slavery. Henry Stanton, rapidly becoming the leader of his group, incurred the wrath of Garrison in the process.

One lovely morning Henry Stanton joined Elizabeth Cady on the patio after breakfast. "As we have no conventions on hand, what do you say to a ride on horseback this morning?"

"That would be fun," Elizabeth agreed, and the two were off for a long ride On the way home they stopped often to admire the autumn hues—and each other. As they passed through a quiet grove, Henry Stanton paused, then suddenly revealed his feelings for her. Elizabeth, flushed with pleasure, agreed to marry this man, ten years her senior, and join with him in the antislavery cause.

The happy couple were eager to share their news with Cousin Gerrit. To their surprise, his reaction was not exactly favorable.

"I feel responsible for this engagement," he told Elizabeth in the privacy of his library, "because the whole series of events transpired while you were my guest. Henry is as fine a young man as you would ever meet. I have nothing but admiration and respect for him. I do not doubt that the two of you are well suited to each other. But you know how conservative families such as yours feel about the whole antislavery movement and abolitionists in particular. The aversion your father feels for Henry's work and goals will prevent his ever approving such a marriage. He will never consent."

"Oh, Cousin Gerrit!" Elizabeth asked, " what can we do to win him over?"

26

Gerrit Smith replied with a lengthy lecture on love, friendship, and marriage. He felt it his duty to present all the pitfalls of the matrimonial state, urging Elizabeth to consider all aspects of her life. She felt her initial glow of happiness change slowly to dismay. She was not so much troubled by Cousin Gerrit's lecture, delivered, she realized, from a sense of duty, as she was with the possibility of confrontation with her father, and with the sinking realization that once more she would fail to please him.

"Is there any way to convince my father?" she asked again.

"My advice," replied Cousin Gerrit, "would be to announce your engagement by letter so that you can remain in Peterboro while Daniel's wrath has a chance to subside."

Elizabeth readily agreed. But Judge Cady did not even bother to answer her letter. He reasoned that he could talk some sense into his daughter when she returned home.

The glorious autumn of 1839 faded. Back in Johnstown, Elizabeth faced her father and another dissertation on marriage, this time from a financial perspective. Elizabeth was perplexed after hearing Cousin Gerrit and her father. Before, her only real fears had been of death and eternity; now she became apprehensive about her future on earth. Marriage, it seemed, would be the most serious step she would take in her life. She resented what Judge Cady and Cousin Gerrit had done. "How little," she later wrote, "strong men, with their logic, sophistry, and hypothetical examples, appreciate the violence they inflict on the tender sensibilities of a woman's heart, in trying to subjugate her to their will!"

The doubts continued. Should she exchange her free

27

and joyous girlhood for an uncertain future? Did she dare oppose the wishes of her family? Even her friends, who had formerly painted rosy pictures of marriage, now tried to dissuade her. Edward Bayard was the most opposed of all. Again he begged her to go away with him; again she refused. She loved Edward and she loved Henry, too. She knew she could never marry Edward. Why was everyone so opposed to her marriage with Henry? She was greatly disturbed by the scenes her friends described: men were untrustworthy tyrants. She remembered the women who had come to her father's law office, the unequal position of married women before the law. Was she wise to take such a step?

Only Henry's frequent letters sustained her. His eloquent and tender promises of a bright future for them countered Judge Cady's dire predictions. He wrote of his stable financial condition. He could indeed support her on his salary as a newspaper correspondent and antislavery lecturer. "Since I was thirteen years old," he wrote, "I have been thrown entirely upon my own resources, especially as to money." In the same letter he established his direct descent from Elder Brewster of the *Mayflower*.[6] Judge Cady could certainly not attack his family background.

However, the pressure became too great. Elizabeth gave in to her family and friends and broke her engagement. Undaunted, Henry sought to change her mind. He wrote that he would be leaving in May to attend the World's Anti-Slavery Convention in London. Elizabeth must marry him and accompany him to Europe.

Elizabeth could not bear the thought of an ocean between herself and Henry. She was twenty-five years old and would no longer be treated as a child. She changed her mind again and agreed to marry him. The Cadys reluctantly began hasty preparations for a small family wedding and the journey. The date was set for Thursday, May 10, 1840, but Henry Stanton's boat was detained by a bar in the North River. They persuaded the pastor to go ahead with the ceremony on Friday, a day commonly held to be bad luck for marriages. (A happy marriage that lasted nearly half a century disproved that old superstition.) Even more difficult for Elizabeth was convincing the good minister to omit the word "obey" from the marriage service. "I refuse," she argued, "to obey anyone with whom I am entering into an equal relationship." The pastor yielded. In a simple white dress, Elizabeth Cady was wed to Henry B. Stanton. The minister drew out the prayers and a sermon on marriage for an hour. Henry, who had never before seen the Reverend Hugh Maire and his strange pulpit mannerisms, had to struggle to maintain his composure during the performance.

Elizabeth's younger sister Madge, the one member of the family who had stood by her in her decision, accompanied the newlyweds to New York. There she, along with Daniel and Harriet Cady Eaton, bid them farewell. To Elizabeth, the voyage represented the close of one chapter in her life and the beginning of another.

CHAPTER TWO

On board the *Montreal* Elizabeth discussed abolition with her husband and James G. Birney, his fellow delegate to the World's Anti-Slavery Convention. Birney, a southerner who had emancipated his slaves, was the antislavery candidate for the United States presidency.[7] Proper and polished in his own comportment, he relentlessly criticized Elizabeth's high-spirited manners, attempting to tone them down somewhat before they reached England. One evening as they played chess, Elizabeth asked, "Well, what have I said or done today open to criticism?"

"You went to the masthead in a chair, which I think very unladylike. I heard you call your husband 'Henry' in the presence of strangers, which is not permissible in polite society. You should always say 'Mr. Stanton.' You have taken three moves back in this game."

"Bless me!" laughed Elizabeth. "What a catalogue in one day. I fear my mentor will despair of my ultimate perfection."

"I should have more hope if you seemed to feel my rebukes more deeply," replied Birney, "but you evidently think them of too little consequence to be much disturbed by them."

During the eighteen-day voyage, he also called attention to minor flaws in Henry's character. "Never fear,"

Elizabeth consoled her husband. "We are as nearly perfect as mortals need be for the wear and tear of ordinary life."

"Yes," Henry agreed with a smile. "Birney is overly critical at times."

When they landed, the couple was struck by the beauty of the English countryside in early June. In Exeter, Elizabeth mused, "Can one wonder at the power of the Catholic religion for centuries, with such accessories to stimulate the imagination to a blind worship of the unknown?"

In London their Queen Street lodginghouse, which had seemed gloomy, came to life when the delegation of American women arrived. Elizabeth was happy to renew old friendships and to meet many new allies: Ann Green Phillips, who, like her husband Wendell, was active in the antislavery cause; Lydia Maria Child, a well-known writer from Massachusetts who had turned all her efforts toward the abolition movement; and Angelina and Sarah Grimké, daughters of a wealthy southern planter. (The sisters had fled to Philadelphia as a result of their strong conviction against slavery.) Elizabeth was especially pleased to see Lucretia Mott, whose liberal ideas were to prove a challenge.

Once again, Elizabeth learned, the ranks of the antislavery movement were divided: this time the issue was whether or not women had the right to speak and vote within the convention. Opposing the views of James Birney, her husband, and other gradualists, Elizabeth, along with the Garrisonians, believed the women should be granted their rights. She argued with Henry, "There is no question so important as the emancipation of women from the dogmas of the past, political, social, and religious. How can the abolitionists, who feel so keenly the wrongs of the slave, be so oblivious to the equal wrongs of their own mothers, wives, and sisters? According to common law, both classes occupy a similar legal status."

When the World's Anti-Slavery Convention opened on June 12, 1840, in Freemason's Hall in London, women were denied the right to participate as delegates even though many represented American antislavery groups composed entirely of females. The debate over their participation raged all day. To Elizabeth's great pride and pleasure, Henry reversed his position and spoke eloquently on behalf of the women. Much of the opposition, she thought, was shallow reasoning. The English clergymen, Bibles in hand, insisted that the subjection of women was divinely ordained when Eve had been created. George Bradburn, hulking head and shoulders above almost every other man present, thundered his refutation:

If anyone can prove to me that the Bible teaches the subjection of one half the human race to the other, then the best thing I could do for humanity would be to bring together every Bible in the universe and make a great bonfire of them.

The most dramatic moment of the convention occurred when the great William Lloyd Garrison scorned the other delegates, joining the women in their seats behind a low curtain.

After battling so many long years for the liberties of African slaves [he announced], I can take no part in a convention that strikes down the most sacred rights of all women. All of the slaves are not men.

The women present never forgot that act of sacrifice by

the man who had been so eager to participate in the convention.

As Elizabeth left the proceedings that day, she heard many remark, "It is about time some demand is made for new liberties for women." She discussed the idea with Lucretia Mott, who was some twenty years older than she and a liberal thinker who questioned religion, politics, and social reform. Her refusal to interpret the Scriptures literally or to accept any man-made creed impressed Elizabeth, who still feared theological dogma even as she rebelled against it.

At every opportunity Elizabeth talked with the Quaker woman and, on one occasion, went to hear her preach in a Unitarian Church. Although she had never before heard a woman speak in public, Elizabeth believed that every woman had the right to do so and should be encouraged to exercise that right.

"When we return home," Elizabeth resolved, "we must hold a convention and form a society to advance the rights of women." Lucretia readily agreed and offered to help with the necessary plans.

In addition to attending the convention, Elizabeth and Henry managed to enjoy all the sights in London, from the dome of St. Paul's Cathedral to the tunnel just excavated under the Thames. They visited museums, prisons, hospitals, art galleries, theaters, churches, and parks. Up and down the Thames they sailed, talking over all the sights and the convention as well. They laughed about their friend James Birney: he had opposed the seating of female delegates at the sessions so vehemently that it had been necessary for him to seek new lodging in order to avoid facing the angry women each day.

As the convention ended, Elizabeth renewed her

34

determination to combat the social stigma against her sex. None of the pleasures of sightseeing nor of stimulating dinner conversations with extraordinary people could make her forget the bitter experience of the women at the convention.

Accompanied by some of the other delegates, Elizabeth and Henry journeyed to Paris. For a month they toured about, enjoying the city and its environs. One of the sights that most impressed Elizabeth was the Hôtel des Invalides as it was being prepared for the remains of Napoleon. Frequently, they saw Louis Philippe in his carriage: Elizabeth recalled that while he had been an exile in the United States, he had taught school. "What an honor for Yankee children to have been taught, by a French king, the rudiments of his language," she remarked to Henry. The gay Sundays in Paris contrasted with the solemnity of that day in the United States. Elizabeth was pleased to see many families in the museums, concert halls, libraries, and parks.

Because Henry and James Birney had arranged to lecture on slavery throughout the British Isles, they returned to travel through England, Scotland, and Ireland, visiting the birthplaces of Shakespeare and Burns and the home of Oliver Cromwell. Alone together for the first time since their marriage, the couple spent a few days in Scotland, walking among the lakes and mountains, riding donkeys, and sailing on Loch Katrine and Loch Lomond.

Ireland was suffering through a period of severe famine, and Elizabeth was appalled by the destitute state of great numbers of people there. "I can not believe," she told her husband, "that poverty is a necessary link in the human experience, that it must

35

always be just because it has always been." In Dublin they dined one evening with the Irish nationalist and labor leader Daniel O'Connell. Elizabeth, who respected him greatly for his support of the women at the London convention, asked, "Do you hope to succeed with your Repeal of the Union measure?"[8]

"No," he replied, "but it is always good to claim the uttermost and then you will be sure to get something." Elizabeth never forgot this advice.

Wherever they went, she quickly became involved in a heated discussion of woman's rights. On Christmas Eve, when she and Henry returned to New York, she was glad to be home and eager to begin the work she had set for herself. Life seemed to offer new purpose.

The Stantons journeyed to Johnstown where Elizabeth was surprised to see that everything seemed much the same as it had always been. In fact, the only change to occur in the ten months of her absence, she felt, was in herself—and that was notable. Because Henry decided to study law with Judge Cady, the young couple made their home for the next two years with Elizabeth's family. She occupied her time reading law, history, and political economy and attended occasional temperance or antislavery meetings. As she learned more about the position of women in history and religion, Elizabeth wrote her findings to Lucretia Mott:

The more I think on the present condition of woman, the more I am oppressed with the reality of her degradation. The laws of our country, how unjust they are! Our customs, how vicious! What God has made sinful, both in man and woman, custom has made sinful in women alone.[9]

For a time, however, it was necessary to postpone all thoughts of organizing to work for improved conditions for women. Elizabeth was now expecting a baby.

CHAPTER THREE

On March 2, 1842, Daniel Cady Stanton was born. Elizabeth turned her energies to the problems of child care, a subject on which scientific thought would not be focused for years to come. She observed to Henry, distressed, "If we buy a plant of a horticulturist we ask him many questions as to its needs, whether it thrives best in sunshine or in shade, whether it needs much or little water, what degrees of heat or cold; but when we hold in our arms for the first time, a being of infinite possibilities, in whose wisdom may rest the destiny of a nation, we take it for granted that the laws governing its life, health, and happiness are intuitively understood, that there is nothing new to be learned in regard to it."

Elizabeth soon learned that many of the common practices of the day were not beneficial to babies, and that some of them were actually harmful. Theodore and Angelina Grimké Weld had warned her that, of all the available literature on child care, only Andrew Combe's *Infancy* was reliable.

The nurse helping Elizabeth refused to listen to her ideas. When Elizabeth insisted that her child not be tightly bound in cloths, the nurse replied that she would not take the responsibility of nursing a baby without a bandage.

"Well," Elizabeth rejoined, "sit down, dear nurse, and

let us reason together. Do not think that I am setting up my judgment against yours, with all your experience. I am simply trying to act on the opinions of a distinguished physician, who says there should be no pressure on a child anywhere: that the limbs and body should be free; that it is cruel to bandage or constrain an infant. Can you give me one good reason why a child should be bound?"

"Yes! I can give you a dozen."

"I only asked for one," Elizabeth goaded.

The nurse hesitated. "Well, the bones of a newborn infant are soft, like cartilage, and unless you pin them up snugly, there is danger of their falling apart."

"It seems to me," reasoned Elizabeth, "that you have given the strongest reason why they should be carefully guarded against the slightest pressure. It is very remarkable that kittens and puppies should be so well put together that they need no artificial bracing, and the human family be left wholly to the mercy of a bandage. Suppose a child was born where you could not get a bandage. What then? Now, I think this child will remain intact without a bandage. If I am willing to take the risk, why should you complain?"

"Because if the child should die, it would injure my name as a nurse. I wash my hands of all these newfangled notions!"

Every morning the nurse carefully bound the baby, and every morning Elizabeth removed the bandage. She refused to allow the nurse to give the child herbs for colic or "insomnia." She insisted on opening the blinds to let the sunshine stream into the nursery, refused to let the baby wear a cap indoors, and requested the nurse to stop singing mournful hymns around young Daniel.

"If you stop giving the baby all those concoctions

and keep the room at sixty-five degrees," Elizabeth insisted, "he will regulate his own sleep."

"I can not sit in a room at such a low temperature."

"Well," said Elizabeth, "sit in the next room and regulate the heat to suit yourself. When I need your services, I will ring a bell!"

When Daniel was six weeks old, the nurse left, confessing that she had indeed learned some valuable lessons.

Elizabeth's firm belief in her own reasoned approach to motherhood brought her into conflict with doctors too. She discovered soon after Daniel's birth that he had a bent collarbone. The physician applied pressure to the shoulder and anchored the bandage to the baby's wrist. He instructed Elizabeth to leave it that way for ten days. Elizabeth soon discovered the tiny hand turning blue because of impeded circulation. "Take the bandage off," she ordered the nurse.

"No, indeed," the nurse replied firmly. I shall never interfere with the doctor."

Elizabeth took it off herself and called in another physician. He replaced the bandage but fastened it to the child's hand rather than to the wrist. Elizabeth, upon noticing the fingers turning blue, removed that bandage also.

"What a woman!" the nurse exclaimed. "Now what do you propose to do?"

"Think out something better myself. Now, what we want is a little pressure on the collarbone. The question is, how can we get it without involving the arm?"

"I am sure I don't know," the nurse answered nervously.

Elizabeth thought for a few minutes. Then she placed a wet strip of linen on the collarbone and anchored it with two linen bands, which she crisscrossed in front and back and pinned to the baby's diaper. In ten days, when the two physicians returned, they both pronounced the baby cured.

Elizabeth told them what she had done. Smiling at each other, they said, "Well, after all, a mother's instinct is better than a man's reason."

"Thank you, gentlemen," retorted Elizabeth, " there was no instinct about it. I did some hard thinking before I saw how to get pressure on the shoulder without impeding the circulation, as you did."

She later wrote, "I trusted neither men nor books absolutely after this, either in regard to the heavens above or the earth beneath, but continued to use my 'mother's instinct,' if 'reason' is too dignified a term to apply to a woman's thoughts."

Contrary to the practice of her day, Elizabeth Cady Stanton refused to spank a child for crying; she believed that, when a baby cried, there had to be a reason. Nor would she give opium, the common sedative of the time. "To spank it for crying is to silence the watchman on the tower through fear," she reasoned. "To give soothing syrup is to drug the watchman while the evils go on." Most of her thinking about child care has since been verified by medical science.

In the fall of 1843 Henry Stanton began to practice law in Boston. Once again Elizabeth found herself in the stimulating company of such reformers as Elizabeth Peabody, Lydia Maria Child, and Oliver Johnson. There she met John Greenleaf Whittier, Theodore Parker, Ralph Waldo Emerson, James Russell Lowell, Nathaniel Hawthorne, John Pierpont, Parker Pillsbury—most of the leading thinkers and crusaders of the day. She attended dinners at the William Lloyd Garrison home,

40

lectures and antislavery meetings, concerts and the theater.

Oliver Johnson escorted Elizabeth to a lecture series at the Marlborough Chapel given by Theodore Parker. This was not long after the well-known minister had shocked even his fellow Unitarians by his famous sermon, "The Permanent and Transient in Religion." He had denied the validity of miracles in the Bible and was no longer allowed to preach in Unitarian pulpits. Elizabeth later wrote, "Reading Theodore Parker's lectures years afterward, I was surprised to find how little there was in them to shock anybody—the majority of thinking people having grown up to them."

Eighteen forty-three was also the year that Judge Cady went to Albany to establish two of his sons-in-law in the legal profession. Elizabeth spent several winters with her family in the New York capital, actively involved in the discussions of the Married Women's Property bill pending before the legislature. The bill was first introduced in 1836 and finally passed in 1848. It was supported, not by women, but by wealthy Dutch farmers who did not want their property squandered by sons-in-law.

In Albany in March 1844 Elizabeth's second son, Henry, was born. This time she felt even more confident of her ability to care for a child. She soon returned to Boston, to a lovely new home in Chelsea, overlooking Boston Bay. Her husband told her, "Since business is taking almost all my time, you must take complete charge of the housekeeping."

Elizabeth laughed, "I feel like a young minister must feel when he takes charge of his first congregation." She studied domestic economics and read all she could find about running a household. Working alongside her servants, she did chores herself; she did not simply supervise them. This was, at least in part, because her help was needed. "Even washing day—that day so many people dread—had its charms for me," she wrote. "The clean clothes on the lines and the grass looked so white and smelled so sweet, that it was to me a pretty sight to contemplate. I inspired my laundress with an ambition to have her clothes look white and to get them out earlier than our neighbors, and to have them ironed and put away sooner."She experimented gaily with cooking, preserving, and pickling. Her compulsion for order and cleanliness was such that she paid to have the firewood piled with the smooth ends of the logs turned outward. She was as caught up in her domestic duties as a child with a new doll house.

In September 1845, Gerrit Smith Stanton joined the growing family.

In spite of her busy life, Elizabeth continued to find great pleasure in reading. She loved the volume of Whittier's poems published in 1838 and "Dedicated to Henry B. Stanton, as a token of the author's personal friendship, and of his respect for the unreserved devotion of exalted talents to the cause of humanity and freedom." From the shelf she took down a volume she had bought in Edinburgh and not yet read: *Records of Woman* by Mrs. Hemans, a series of poems in honor of women.

The intellectual and cultural atmosphere of Boston stimulated her and buoyed her spirits. But the winter climate was too severe for her husband's delicate health, and so, in the spring of 1847, the Stantons moved to Seneca Falls, New York. In the vicinity lived a large circle of reformers, including William Henry Channing and Frederick Douglass at Rochester and Elizabeth's cousin Gerrit Smith at Peterboro. Elizabeth, however, was to be totally occupied.

The new house had not been lived in for five years, and weeds had overtaken the five acres of land. Handing his daughter a check, Judge Cady had challenged: "You believe in woman's capacity to do and dare: now go ahead and put your house in order."

As Elizabeth had left her three boys with her mother, she accepted the challenge. With a team of workers, she spent more than a month preparing the house for her family. Her neighbor, Ansel Bascom, a member of the constitutional convention then meeting in Albany, came by often to advise her about the remodeling project. They sat on boxes, watching the progress of the workmen and talking about the status of women. On one occasion Elizabeth urged him to eliminate the word "male" from the suffrage clause in the State Constitution.

"I agree with you that women should have political equality," he replied, "but I am not willing to make myself the laughingstock of the convention."

Elizabeth found the change from her active life in Boston depressing. The Stanton home was located on the outskirts of town, and the roads were often muddy. Frequently, Henry was away on business. Also, Elizabeth felt that the servants failed to meet her high standards, and her three growing boys were constantly needing new clothes and always getting into mischief. Housekeeping was no longer a novelty. Indeed, she found most of her routine irksome. Later she wrote, "I suffered with mental hunger. I had books, but no stimulating companionship. The love of order and the beautiful and artistic all seemed fading away in the struggle to accomplish what was absolutely necessary

43

from hour to hour."

As she reflected on her increasingly tedious life and the condition of women in general, Elizabeth wondered if community living or a cooperative household arrangement would not be better than an isolated family life. Looking back on the period, she remembered, "The general discontent I felt with woman's portion as wife, mother, housekeeper, physician, and spiritual guide, the chaotic conditions into which everything fell without her constant supervision, and the wearied, anxious look of the majority of women impressed me with a strong feeling that some active measures should be taken to remedy the wrongs of society in general, and of women in particular."

Elizabeth found herself thinking more and more about woman's problems. To her friend Rebecca Eyster, she wrote,

> I have very serious objections, dear Rebecca, to being called Henry. Ask our colored brethren if there is nothing in a name. Why are the slaves nameless unless they take that of their master? Simply because they have no independent existence. They are mere chattels, with no civil or social rights. Even so with women. The custom of calling women Mrs. John This and Mrs. Tom That, and colored men Sambo and Zip Coon, is founded on the principle that white men are the lords of all.[10]

In April 1848 the Married Women's Property bill finally passed the New York legislature. Now a married woman could own real estate in her own right. Reflecting on the women who had come to her father's law office so many years ago, Elizabeth rejoiced that things would be different for their daughters.

44

CHAPTER FOUR

Frequently Elizabeth's thoughts returned to London of 1840 and her discussions with Lucretia Mott. They had talked of organizing women to work for their rights, of holding a convention to discuss the problems women faced. But eight years had passed, and Lucretia was in Philadelphia, a long distance from Seneca Falls in the nineteenth century.

Then, in July of 1848, Elizabeth received happy news: Lucretia was visiting with her sister in nearby Waterloo, New York. Could Elizabeth come to see her there? Martha C. Wright, Lucretia's sister, was also interested in women's rights. Together with their friends Jane Hunt and Mary McClintock, the women decided to form some kind of society. "Why not call a convention now?" Elizabeth asked. "We have waited long enough."

On July 14 their unsigned call to a convention was published in the *Seneca County Courier*:

A convention to discuss the social, civil, and religious condition and rights of women will be held in the Wesleyan Chapel, at Seneca Falls, New York, on Wednesday and Thursday, the 19th and 20th of July current; commencing at 10 o'clock a.m. During the first day the meeting will be exclusively for women, who are earnestly invited to attend. The public generally are invited to be present on the second day, when Lucretia Mott, of Philadelphia, and other ladies and gentlemen, will address the convention.[11]

Time was short. On Sunday they met at the McClintock home to write resolutions and discuss their speeches. They looked over reports from temperance and anti-slavery conventions for ideas, and after many false starts, someone suggested using the Declaration of Independence as a model. As they worked together, the women soon realized that Elizabeth was the best writer among them. She revised the Declaration of Sentiments: "We hold these truths to be self-evident, that all men and women are created equal." A list of eighteen resolutions would be presented. Elizabeth had been thinking about one in particular, which later became the ninth on the list. Eagerly, she read it to Lucretia Mott: "Resolved, That it is the duty of the women of this country to secure to themselves their sacred right to the elective franchise."

To Elizabeth's amazement, Lucretia objected strongly, "Why, Lizzie, thee will make us ridiculous."

"But, Lucretia," Elizabeth persisted, "the power to make the laws is the right through which we can secure all other rights."

Even Henry tried to dissuade her. He threatened to leave town if she presented the resolution, and when the time came, he carried out his threat![12] Finally, she turned to the abolitionist leader and ex-slave, Frederick Douglass, who had come to realize the power of the ballot through his long struggle for freedom for his people. He agreed to support her.

The historic moment arrived. She herself spoke in favor of the Declaration of Sentiments, as did Elizabeth and Mary McClintock, Martha C. Wright, her neighbor

46

Ansel Bascom, and Samuel Tillman, a young law student. Elizabeth was quite happy at the conclusion of the first day's proceedings. It was gratifying to see many women express their opinions. Nevertheless, she began to fear that they would not support her resolution. Perhaps Lucretia, Henry, and the others had been right. Was she indeed being foolish?

The next day a heated debate followed the reading of her revolutionary proposal. Many of the people present feared that it would draw attention away from the other resolutions and that it might embarrass their growing movement. But Frederick Douglass, true to his promise, spoke eloquently of the power of the ballot and the need for all oppressed groups to be able to use the political process. Elizabeth, to her own surprise, was able to speak persuasively on the issue. Finally, although the other resolutions had been adopted unanimously, Elizabeth's was carried by only a narrow margin.

Public reaction to the printed proceedings of the convention shocked the women who had organized it. What they believed to be rational and timely demands were sarcastically ridiculed by the press. Only the antislavery papers (including Frederick Douglass's *The North Star*) supported their action. So intense was the general disfavor that many of the one hundred men and women who had signed the Declaration of Sentiments withdrew their names.

Nevertheless, the ground had been broken. No amount of condemnation could negate the importance of that first step in Seneca Falls. The rights demanded at that small convention included almost everything for which women have been petitioning in the more than a century since: equal rights in the trades, professions, universities, political offices, churches; the right to vote, to make contracts, to sue and be sued, to testify in court; equality in marriage; personal freedom, property, wages. Today some of these rights have not yet been established in law or custom. But Elizabeth Cady Stanton had raised the questions. Promptly, women began to work for the goals established at Seneca Falls.

Another convention was called for August 2 at the Unitarian Church in Rochester. Elizabeth was apprehensive about attending; the reaction of even her closest friends to the Seneca Falls meeting had left her deeply troubled. She did go, but was among those firmly opposed to letting a woman chair the convention. As it happened, Abigail Bush was elected to the position and performed so capably that Elizabeth ashamedly resolved: "Never again will I suggest that women are incapable of any public task!"

Women's rights soon came to occupy a central place in her concerns as new challenges replaced domestic boredom. Elizabeth began using her pen to urge others to consider the issues. In September she wrote to George G. Cooper, editor of the Rochester *National Reformer*,

If God has assigned a sphere to man and one to woman, we claim the right ourselves to judge of His design in reference to us, and we accord to man the same privilege. We think that a man has quite enough to do to find out his own individual calling, without being taxed to find out also where every woman belongs.[13]

In spite of the derision the women encountered, Elizabeth was encouraged by the public attention their conventions were attracting. To Lucretia Mott she wrote,

The publicity given to our ideas . . . will start women thinking, and men too; and when men and women think about a new question, the first step in progress is taken.[14]

The movement spread. Various state conventions were organized, and Elizabeth wrote challenging letters to many of them. The busy months flew past, and soon she was awaiting the birth of another child. On February 10, 1851, Theodore Stanton was born, and the following day Elizabeth wrote to her cousin, Elizabeth Smith Miller:

Laugh in your turn. I have actually got my fourth son! Yes, Theodore Stanton bounded upon the stage of life with great ease—comparatively!! He weighs ten and one-half pounds. I was sick but a few hours, and did not lie down until half an hour before he was born, but worked round as hard as I could all night to do up the last things. At seven o'clock Sunday morning he was born. This morning I got up, bathed myself in cold water, and have sat by the table writing several letters.[15]

Two days later she wrote to Henry, who was away on business,

I am regarded as a perfect wonder. Many people are actually impatiently waiting for me to die in order to make their theories good. But I am getting better and stronger every day.[16]

Elizabeth considered pregnancy a natural occurrence, not a disease. She refused to pamper herself, but got plenty of exercise to insure an easy delivery and a rapid recovery. The ideas of her time on obstetrics and pediatrics made no more sense to her than the prevailing views on the role of women.

CHAPTER FIVE

May 1851 marked the beginning of the half-century long association between Elizabeth and her friend and partner Susan Brownell Anthony. It was a turning point in Elizabeth's life and an event significant in the history of the woman's rights movement. Elizabeth was to be the writer-philosopher, Susan the organizer. Working enthusiastically for the cause in which they both believed so strongly, they would complement each other perfectly. Rarely in history has a team collaborated more effectively.

Susan B. Anthony, daughter of a Quaker family, had long been active in temperance and antislavery causes. About 1850, disenchanted with her job teaching in the academy at Canajoharie, New York, she had turned her attention toward reforms. First reports of the woman's rights conventions amused her, and she failed to take the idea seriously. As she heard and thought more about the movement, however, the women's demands seemed to follow logically the very principles on which the Republic was founded.

In May 1851 antislavery lecturers George Thompson and William Lloyd Garrison were guests in the Stanton home while attending a convention in Seneca Falls. Walking home after one of the meetings, Elizabeth met her friend Amelia Bloomer, and with her was Susan B.

Anthony. Having heard much about Elizabeth Cady Stanton, Susan was eager to meet her. Elizabeth immediately liked this woman, five years her junior. Later she remarked, "Why I did not at once invite her home with me to dinner, I do not know. I suppose my mind was full of what I had heard, or my coming dinner, or the probable behavior of three mischievous boys who had been busily exploring the premises while I was at the meeting."

Elizabeth's sons were always into some sort of trouble. Young Henry rigged up a life preserver of corks and decided to test it on his eighteen-month-old brother. Along with his friends, he wheeled the baby in his carriage to the Seneca River, took off the child's clothes, and tied the cork ring under his arms. From a rowboat the boys gleefully watched young Gerrit splash about the river. He was blue with cold when a frantic Elizabeth finally rescued him.

The very next day a neighbor spied the poor toddler perched on the chimney on the highest peak of the roof. Quickly the neighbor went to the child's rescue. A few years later young Gerrit joined his older brothers in locking up Theodore, the youngest, in the smokehouse. Elizabeth punished the trio by shutting them up in the attic, which had only two barred windows. Somehow they kicked them out, slid down the lightning rod, and escaped to the barn. "This," Elizabeth later wrote, "is a fair sample of the quiet happiness I enjoyed in the first years of motherhood."

Susan B. Anthony was a great help to Elizabeth during these trying years. Together they began to write speeches for antislavery and temperance conventions as well as for woman's rights meetings. Elizabeth told Susan, "We must accept every invitation to speak on every question in order to maintain woman's right to do so." Susan agreed. In order to free her friend for writing, Susan helped Elizabeth with her domestic chores and with supervising the boys. She and young Henry were frequently at odds over his mischief-making. "It is pleasant to remember," Elizabeth said later, "that he never seriously injured any of his victims, and only once came near fatally shooting himself with a pistol. The ball went through his hand; happily, a brass button prevented it from penetrating his heart."

It was Susan, also, who spurred Elizabeth on during those years whenever the young mother felt weighted down with her domestic responsibilities. When the day's chores were done and the children finally asleep, the two women sat by the fireplace plotting some new attack in their ceaseless battle to improve the condition of women. "Susan," wrote Elizabeth, "supplied the facts and statistics, I the philosophy and rhetoric, and, together, we have made arguments that have stood unshaken through the storms of long years; arguments that no one has answered."

During these years a great controversy arose about a new form of dress, the bloomer costume. Elizabeth Smith Miller was the first to wear the outfit. During the winter of 1851 she visited Elizabeth Cady Stanton, wearing a short skirt over full-length black broadcloth trousers, a matching Spanish knee-length cloak, a beaver hat with feathers, and dark furs.

"It is simply perfect!" Elizabeth exclaimed as she watched her cousin mount the stairs, a lamp in one hand and a baby in the other. "I cannot carry either one up the stairs with these heavy skirts to manage."

"You, too, must wear one," Elizabeth Smith Miller urged.

It was hardly necessary to urge her. Elizabeth put on a similar outfit the next day. "What incredible freedom!" she exclaimed. "I feel like a captive set free from his ball and chain." Walking was now a pleasure in any sort of weather. Household tasks and gardening became much less difficult.

Elizabeth's friend Amelia Bloomer, who for a time had been deputy postmaster in Seneca Falls, was editor of the *Lily*, a reform journal that advocated temperance and woman's rights. In the journal, Amelia opened a discussion of women's clothing and the new costume; soon, it bore her name. The press ridiculed the idea of women in trousers even though most people agreed that the skirt and petticoats women wore were cumbersome and unhealthy. In the streets crowds of boys would taunt the women who wore this new costume, and people would chant:

> Heigh! ho! in rain and snow,
> The bloomer now is all the go.
> Twenty tailors take the stitches,
> Twenty women wear the breeches.
> Heigh! ho! in rain or snow,
> The bloomer now is all the go.

Elizabeth Smith Miller's father encouraged her to wear practical garments. To Gerrit Smith, the whole question of a more liberated position for women centered on clothes: long skirts were degrading, and if women wanted more freedom, they should stop wearing clothes that constricted their bodies. Susan B. Anthony adopted the bloomer outfit, as did Paulina Wright Davis, Lucy Stone, the Grimké sisters, Dr. Harriet Austin, and others.

The criticism never abated. Elizabeth wrote to Henry at one point,

> There is some question about my going to Johnstown, for Cousin Gerrit says that papa is so distressed about my dress. However, I have written to them that if my friends cannot see me in the short dress, they cannot see me at all.[17]

There is no evidence that Henry, who at the time was serving in the New York State Senate, opposed Elizabeth's new clothing.

But Elizabeth did receive a letter from her son Daniel, away at school, requesting that she not wear a bloomer outfit when she came there to visit. "You do not wish me to visit you in a short dress," she wrote back.

> Why, my dear child, I have no other. Why do you wish me to wear what is uncomfortable, inconvenient, and many times dangerous? I'll tell you why. You want me to be like other people. You do not like to have me laughed at. You must learn not to care for what foolish people say.[18]

After about two years, however, the pressures became too great. Most of the bloomer-wearers began to feel that the controversy over their clothing detracted attention from far more important matters, and so they returned to customary dress. Elizabeth Smith Miller, undaunted, wore the costume for seven trying years.

Family cares, Elizabeth felt, continued to consume far too much of her time, and she was now expecting another child. Even though in the 1850s it was considered improper for a pregnant woman to be seen in public, she continued to receive many invitations to address various conventions and tried to respond as best she could. A temperance convention in Albany in early 1852 had denied women delegates the right to speak. They therefore had withdrawn and had called a Woman's State Temperance Convention for April 20 in Rochester. On April 2 Elizabeth wrote to her friend,

Oh, Susan! Susan! Susan! You must manage to spend a week with me before the Rochester convention, for I am afraid I cannot attend it; I have so much care with all these boys on my hands. But I will write a letter. How much I do long to be free from housekeeping and children, so as to have some time to read, and think, and write. But it may be well for me to understand all the trials of woman's lot, that I may more eloquently proclaim them when the time comes.[19]

Elizabeth was able to attend the convention after all, and was elected president. Her acceptance speech was stirring:

How my heart throbs to see women assembling in convention to inquire what part they have in the great moral struggles of humanity! [she told the delegates.] Verily a new era is dawning upon the world. We shall do much when the pulpit, the forum, the professor's chair, and the ballot box are ours; but the question is, what can we do today?

Among the suggestions she presented were two which evoked severe criticism from the press and the pulpit. "Let no woman remain in the relation of wife with the confirmed drunkard," she implored.

Let no drunkard be the father of her children. . . . Let us petition our State governments so to modify the laws affecting marriage, and the custody of children, that the drunkard shall have no claims on either wife or child.

56

Having attacked marriage and child custody laws, she concluded with a blast at the institutional church:

> In as much as charity begins at home, let us withdraw our mite from all the associations for sending the Gospel to the heathen across the ocean, for the education of young men for the ministry, for the building up of a theological aristocracy and gorgeous temples to the unknown God, and devote ourselves to the poor and suffering about us. ... Good schools and homes ... would do much more to prevent immorality and crime in our cities than all the churches in the land could ever possibly do toward the regeneration of the multitude sunk in poverty, ignorance, and vice.[20]

Unable to appear at the National Woman's Rights Convention in Syracuse the following September, Elizabeth sent a letter, as she was accustomed to do when she could not attend a gathering. She proposed that women who owned property (in states that accorded them that right) refuse to pay taxes as long as they could not vote. She suggested also that coeducation was better than separate schooling for the two sexes. And once again she took up her attack on the church. "Among the clergy we find our most violent enemies—those most opposed to any change in woman's position." Women should direct their time and energies, she concluded, toward "the education, elevation, and enfranchisement of their own sex."[21] The convention discussed her letter at length. Women gradually began to use the strategy of civil disobedience by refusing to pay taxes without representation.

Then, at last, in October 1852, Elizabeth bore her first daughter, Margaret Livingston Stanton. She wrote to Lucretia Mott,

57

She is the largest and most vigorous baby I have ever had, weighing twelve pounds. And yet my labor was short and easy. I laid down about fifteen minutes, and alone with my nurse and one female friend brought forth this big girl. I sat up immediately, changed my own clothes, put on a wet bandage. ... Am I not almost a savage? For what refined, delicate, genteel, civilized woman would get well in so indecently short a time. Dear me, how much cruel bondage of mind and suffering of body poor woman will escape when she takes the liberty of being her own physician of both body and soul![22]

With five children to care for now, Elizabeth was fortunate indeed to find an excellent housekeeper in Amelia Willard. This Quaker woman soon became a firm friend and for thirty years served as the mainstay of the Stanton household. Moreover, she put on the bloomer costume and became an ardent supporter of woman's rights. Amelia felt that her best contribution to the cause was helping to care for the Stanton children and running the household, in order to give Elizabeth more free time for her public work. Amelia was a second mother to the children, and Elizabeth was eager to let her know exactly how much her help meant to the Stantons. "You are a treasure, dear friend! All that I have been able to accomplish has been partly your credit."

In February 1854 Elizabeth made her first speech before the New York State Legislature. Its preparation was no easy matter, as she revealed in a letter to Susan B. Anthony:

My Address is not nearly finished; but if I sit up nights, it shall be done in time. .... Yesterday one of the boys shot an arrow into my baby's eye. The eye is safe, but oh! my fright when I saw the blood come and the organ swell, and witnessed her suffering![23]

58

In the midst of her everyday household cares, Elizabeth was concerned about her father. He had read in the Albany newspaper that his daughter was going to speak at the Capitol and promptly sent word for her to stop at Johnstown on her way to Albany.

Late one evening Elizabeth sat down in Judge Cady's study to read her speech to him. Never was she more nervous than before this audience of one. She wanted his approval, fearing his displeasure more than anything else. She knew he was unsympathetic toward the woman's rights movement and deeply disapproved of her role in it. But she threw herself completely into her speech, and as she read, she noticed tears in her father's eyes. "Oh!" she thought. "At last I have touched his heart." She continued more confidently than ever.

When she had finished, Judge Cady said nothing. Elizabeth could hear her own heart beating in the silence of the room. Then, turning toward her, Daniel Cady said, "Surely you have had a happy, comfortable life, with all your wants and needs supplied; and yet that speech fills me with self-reproach; for one might naturally ask, how can a young woman, tenderly brought up, who has had no bitter personal experience, feel so keenly the wrongs of her sex? Where did you learn this lesson?"

"I learned it here, in your office," she replied, "when I was a child, listening to the complaints women made to you. They who have sympathy and imagination to make the sorrows of others their own can readily learn all the hard lessons of life from experiences of others."

"Well, well!" said Judge Cady. "You have made your points clear and strong; but I think I can find you even more cruel laws than those you have quoted."

He made a few suggestions for her speech and looked

59

up other laws for her. It was quite late when father and daughter kissed each other good night. After that Elizabeth never knew how he really felt about the issues. She did know, however, of her father's wish that in public she be well-prepared. Thus, he continued to provide her with legal information whenever she asked.

Elizabeth first delivered her address before the New York State Woman's Rights Convention, which met in Albany on February 14. Susan had fifty thousand copies printed for distribution. When the time arrived for Elizabeth to speak before the legislature, the senate chamber was crowded with onlookers. Most people had never before heard a woman speak in public. Elizabeth, dressed in black silk trimmed with white lace, looked conventionally ladylike. She certainly did not fit the popular image of the woman who was so brazen as to make a public speech.

Boldly and clearly, she pictured the inferior position of woman under the law.

> We have every qualification required by the Constitution, necessary to the legal voter, but the one of sex. We are moral, virtuous, and intelligent, and in all respects quite equal to the proud white man himself, and yet by your laws we are classed with idiots, lunatics, and Negroes; and though we do not feel honored by the place assigned to us, yet, in fact, our legal position is lower than that of either; for the Negro can be raised to the dignity of a voter if he possesses himself of $250; the lunatic can vote in his moments of sanity, and the idiot, too, if he be a male one, and not more than nine-tenths a fool.

She accused the legislature of creating an aristocracy by elevating the sons above the mothers who gave them birth. She demanded for women accused of criminal acts the right to a trial by a jury of their own peers.

Woman as wife bore the burden of even greater discrimination.

> The wife who inherits no property holds about the same legal position that does the slave on the Southern plantation. She can own nothing, sell nothing. She has no right even to the wages she earns; her person, her time, her services are the property of another. She can not testify, in many cases, against her husband. She can get no redress for wrongs in her own name in any court of justice. She can neither sue nor be sued. She is not held morally responsible for any crime committed in the presence of her husband, so completely is her very existence supposed by law to be merged with that of another.

Elizabeth continued to list laws that discriminated against the married woman.

Then she turned to children.

> By your laws, the child is the absolute property of the father, wholly at his disposal in life or death. In case of separation, the law gives the children to the father; no matter what his character or condition.

And what did woman want?

> Let us say, in behalf of the women of this State, we ask for all that you have asked for yourselves, in the progress of your development, since the *Mayflower* cast anchor beside Plymouth Rock; and simply on the ground that the rights of every human being are the same and identical.[24]

Elizabeth sat down, flushed with pride at the applause. She knew that she had done well. Yet the power of her speech and of all the petitions the women presented did not move the legislature to act.

Later, some women came up to congratulate Elizabeth. One of them inquired in a deprecating manner, "But what do you do with your children?"

"Ladies," answered Elizabeth, "it takes me no longer to speak than you to listen; what have you done with your children the two hours you have been sitting here? But, to answer your question, I never leave my children to go to Saratoga, Washington, Newport, or Europe, or even to come here. They are, at this moment, with a faithful nurse at Delevan House. Having accomplished my mission, we shall all return home together."

Elizabeth often heard women say that they objected to the woman's rights movement because it was immodest to speak in public and because the accompanying publicity was in bad taste. She always told them, "Modesty and taste are questions of latitude and education; the more people know—the more their ideas expanded by travel, experience, and observation—the less easily they are shocked. The narrowness and bigotry of women are the result of their circumscribed sphere of thought and action." Women, she was convinced, would work for their rights, only if they could transcend that sphere. She was determined to do what she could to help.

CHAPTER SIX

Not content with advocating suffrage and legal equality for women, Elizabeth Cady Stanton now approached the subject of marriage and divorce. In a letter to Susan B. Anthony in March 1853, she admitted that society might not be willing to discuss the topic. But, she wrote, "it is vain to look for the elevation of woman so long as she is degraded in marriage."

> I hold that it is a sin, an outrage on our holiest feelings, to pretend that anything but deep, fervent love and sympathy constitute marriage. . . . I ask for no laws on marriage. . . . Man in his lust has regulated long enough this whole question of sexual intercourse. Now let the motherhood of mankind . . . rouse up and give this whole matter a thorough, fearless examination.[25]

In November 1856 Elizabeth sent a letter to the National Woman's Rights Convention. She asked how woman could

> endure our present marriage relations, by which woman's life, health, and happiness are held so cheap, that she herself feels that God has given her no charter of rights, no individuality of her own? I answer, she patiently bears all this because in her blindness she sees no way of escape. . . . She looks to heaven, whilst the more philosophical slave sets out for Canada.

Marriage, she insisted, was intended for the happiness of both parties. Woman should not sacrifice her individuality to her role as wife and mother. And, like the slave, the married woman even assumes the name of her master.

> What man can honestly deny that he has not a secret feeling that where his pleasure and woman's seems to conflict, the woman must be sacrificed; and what is worse, woman herself has come to think so, too.[26]

Elizabeth also came to have strong feelings about the need for liberal divorce laws after she witnessed the sufferings of a close friend in whose wedding she had been a bridesmaid. A liberal divorce bill was introduced in the New York legislature and defeated by only four votes. Horace Greeley had strongly opposed the bill in his influential New York *Tribune*, and Elizabeth blamed him for the defeat. Completely convinced that her ideas were right, she believed that any rational person was bound to agree. It never occurred to her that she might be criticized for attacking so venerable an institution as marriage.

In May 1860 the subject of marriage and divorce came up at the Tenth National Woman's Rights Convention. Since the laws differed for men and women, many felt that these were legitimate topics for discussion. Elizabeth presented resolutions and spoke eloquently for more than an hour; then the Reverend Antoinette Brown Blackwell presented a set of opposing resolutions. To Elizabeth's amazement, Wendell Phillips moved that the resolutions and speeches be stricken from the record. The whole discussion, he maintained, was irrelevant to the convention.

Elizabeth turned scarlet with embarrassment at the disapproval by such an esteemed friend. The Reverend Samuel Longfellow, sitting next to her, whispered, "Nevertheless, you are right, and the convention will sustain you." It did; Wendell Phillips's motion lost.

In a letter to the New York *Tribune*, Elizabeth defended her action. She was quite alarmed by the severity of criticism from the press and by a lack of support from other sources as well. Lucy Stone, who in several letters had encouraged her to speak out on the subject, was now strangely silent. She received letters asking such absurd questions as, "What will home life be like when men change wives every Christmas?" Yet she took comfort in letters from women who now had fresh courage to face their tragic lives. She wrote to Susan, "Our religion, laws, customs, are all founded on the belief that woman was made for man. Come what will, my whole soul rejoices in the truth that I have uttered. One word of thanks from a suffering woman outweighs with me the howls of all Christendom."27

Along with public conflicts, there were the usual domestic ups and downs. With all her duties, it was extremely difficult for her to find time to write. There was further conflict with her father. Judge Cady had tried to dissuade her from making any more appearances before the legislature by offering her the deed to a house she wanted. She refused him. Then, during a visit with her at Seneca Falls, he asked, "Elizabeth, are you getting ready to lecture before the lyceums?"

"Yes, sir."

"I hope," threatened the judge, "you will never do it during my lifetime, for if you do, be assured of one thing, your first lecture will be a very expensive one."

"I intend," Elizabeth replied, "that it shall be a

profitable one." They left the room by separate doors. Judge Cady disinherited Elizabeth at that time, but he relented just before his death in October 1859.

Never did Elizabeth feel that she had lived up to her father's expectations even though she knew he respected her courage and determination. She believed that things would have been different had she been born male. "I never felt more keenly the degradation of my sex," she wrote to Susan. "To think that all in me of which my father would have felt a proper pride had I been a man, is deeply mortifying to him because I am a woman."[28] The little girl with her prized Greek Testament was more than just a half-forgotten memory.

Even Henry voiced his opposition, partly because Elizabeth's family felt so strongly that she should not write or speak publicly on the woman question. Away from home much of the time as a political correspondent and writer for New York newspapers and as a member of the New York legislature, Henry wrote several letters home for each one he received from Elizabeth. "You could write much more frequently to me if you did not spend so much time writing speeches and articles," he accused her in a moment of irritation. When something went wrong at home, he sometimes blamed her wider preoccupations, forgetting that his absence also contributed to her burden of familial responsibility.[29]

Out of intense loyalty to Henry, Elizabeth seldom complained about his opposition to her public activities. She wrote to Susan in one of the moments when she was feeling very low, warning her friend that the letter was to be kept strictly confidential, "Sometimes, Susan, I struggle in deep waters." She vowed that she would continue to write and speak. She told her of her plans to write for *The Una*, a new reform paper edited by their friend, Paulina Wright Davis: "A good time is coming and my future is always bright and beautiful."[30]

Henry B. Stanton loved and respected Elizabeth too much to interfere with her efforts. Indeed, he helped edit some of the letters and articles she wrote for publication. He was proud of her abilities and courage, even as he sought to shield her from further criticism. The mutual respect and love with which they had begun their marriage continued to grow, even through long periods of separation.

Five children kept Elizabeth busy enough, but there were more. Harriot Eaton, her second daughter—and a future suffragist—was born January 20, 1856, Robert, her seventh and last child, was born March 14, 1859. That pregnancy was difficult for Elizabeth, and she needed far more than her usual brief time to recuperate. On October 31 of that year her father died after suffering through several months of blindness. This, and the temporary mental breakdown of her beloved Cousin Gerrit Smith following John Brown's trial and execution, saddened her deeply.[31]

But the woman's cause was moving forward, and for the first time with some real financial backing. In 1859 Charles F. Hovey, of Boston, left $50,000 to be spent annually in various reform movements, including woman's rights. One year earlier another Bostonian, Francis Jackson, had given Wendell Phillips $5,000 to be used toward the enfranchisement of women. Typical of the smaller donations which came in from friends of the movement was the draft for twenty-five dollars that Gerrit Smith sent to Elizabeth in May 1860. "To no better cause can money, time, or talents be appropriated," he wrote.[32] Elizabeth, Susan, Lucy Stone, and other women began to organize campaigns to press for woman suffrage.

CHAPTER SEVEN

Then, war! The nation was torn apart by the election of Abraham Lincoln to the presidency and the secession of the southern states. No one remained untouched during the four long, bloody, difficult years that Americans fought Americans. The last Woman's Rights Convention before the war was held in Albany in February 1861. Again, divorce was the principal, and most controversial, topic. During the next five years the women set aside all their efforts—conventions, petitions, and lobbying—and turned to the crisis at hand.

Women on both sides of the lines fought in the ranks until they were discovered, planned military campaigns, gathered and made supplies for the armies, nursed and comforted the wounded and dying, and made countless other little-known contributions to the war effort. Most of those in the North who had for decades worked ardently for reform were also as ardently in favor of the war. They insisted from the beginning, however, that the conflict must be fought to free the slaves, not simply to restore the Union.

Elizabeth Cady Stanton and Susan B. Anthony, after consultation with Horace Greeley, William Lloyd Garrison, and Robert Dale Owen, issued a call for a meeting of women at Cooper Institute, New York, in 1863, to form a Woman's Loyal League. Resolutions adopted at the meeting included one favoring the establishment of civil and political rights for all citizens. The women spent months circulating petitions advocating freedom for slaves.

For once, most of the press supported the women. Horace Greeley's New York *Tribune* editorialized,

The women of the Loyal League have shown great practical wisdom in restricting their efforts to one subject, the most important which any society can aim at in this hour, and great courage in undertaking to do what has never been done in the world before, to obtain one million names to a petition.[33]

When these same women had demanded rights for themselves, they were called imprudent and fanatical. Now they were admirable for their patriotism and executive abilities!

Susan, as a Quaker pacifist, would not support the war. She tried repeatedly to turn Elizabeth's attention back to the issues of woman's rights, but Elizabeth urged her to wait until after the war. Too late, she realized that Susan had been right. In 1862 the New York legislature amended the law for which women had fought so hard in 1860. They removed from women equal right to guardianship of their children and repealed the law guaranteeing a widow control of her deceased husband's property for care and protection of dependent minors.

During the war the Stantons moved from Seneca Falls to New York City. By that time Henry was writing editorials for the New York *Tribune*, and soon he resumed his law practice. When the war was going badly for the Union in the early months, Elizabeth, along with many abolitionists, criticized the policies coming out of

Washington. "I do hope the rebels will sack Washington," she wrote to Elizabeth Smith Miller, "take Lincoln, Seward, and McClellan, and keep them safe in some Southern fort until we man the ship of state with those who know whither they are steering and for what purpose."[34]

The older Stanton boys drilled daily. At age seventeen Henry had run away from home to enlist. The youngest son, Bob, was causing his mother no little difficulty. As he enjoyed throwing rocks, he had broken a few windows, and afterward Elizabeth tried to reason with him.

"Rocks break windows," she said.

"I thought glass was strong," he replied.

"Oh, you hopeless boy! Then I shall pray for you."

"God isn't looking at me," her son informed her. After paying for another broken window, Elizabeth gave up reason as well as prayer and spanked him soundly.

"I won't throw any more rocks," he promised, sobbing. If he did, he was more careful.[35] Elizabeth concluded that it was sometimes necessary to apply reason to the seat of the pants.

In July 1863 the infamous Draft Riots rocked New York City. The Conscription Law permitted a man drafted into the army to hire a substitute for three hundred dollars. Understandably, poor men, who could not afford substitutes, protested the inequity of this law. Unfortunately, they turned their wrath against blacks and abolitionists, and a black orphanage close to the Stanton home (at 75 West Forty-fifth Street) was burned to the ground.

For two days the mob roamed the neighborhood. Elizabeth watched, horrified, as the little children were marched off, two by two, from the burning orphanage.

"A double portion of martyrdom has been meted out to our poor blacks," she commented. "I am led to ask if there is no justice in heaven or on earth that this should be permitted through the centuries." Horace Greeley took refuge at the home of Edward and Tryphena Bayard; the Stantons went there for a night, taking Susan with them.

One night as young Daniel was standing in front of his own house, some rioters grabbed him, "Here's one of those three hundred dollar fellows!" they shouted. Elizabeth, watching, shook with fear for his safety. Daniel used his wits, however, and as the group passed a saloon, shouted, "Let's go in, fellows, and take a drink." He treated all of them, who then demanded that he join them in "three cheers for Jeff Davis." Daniel cheered as enthusiastically as anyone. "Oh, he seems to be a good fellow," said one of the men. "Let 'im go." By deception, Daniel had apparently saved his life.

While her son was in the bar, Elizabeth stayed alone with the other children. Her anguish at seeing him dragged off turned to fear. At any moment the mob might start pounding on her front door. Quickly, she sent the children and servants to the fourth floor. Opening the skylight, she told them, "If we are attacked, run out over the roof to a neighbor's house." Then, in her mind, she formulated a speech, planning if necessary to open the door and appeal to the unruly crowds as American citizens. Just then a police squad and two companies of soldiers appeared on the scene. After a bloody fracas, the rioters were taken off to jail, and quiet returned to the neighborhood.[36]

Quickly Elizabeth left with her children for Johnstown after a shattering experience with what she called the "most brutal mob" she had ever seen.

Elizabeth and her co-workers in the Loyal League, along with all abolitionists, rejoiced when the Emancipation Proclamation was issued. But they believed that a constitutional guarantee against slavery was necessary to complete the work. Elizabeth therefore returned to New York City as soon as it was safe to do so and helped gather one hundred thousand signatures for the emancipation petition she forwarded to Senator Charles Sumner, of Massachusetts, in February 1864. By August, more than 400,000 persons had signed. After the 1864 elections, both houses of Congress passed the Thirteenth Amendment, prohibiting slavery and involuntary servitude within the United States.

Like most other abolitionists, Elizabeth and Henry Stanton supported John C. Fremont over Abraham Lincoln in 1864, agreeing with Wendell Phillips that justice was more important than union.[37] But after he was reelected, Lincoln supported the Thirteenth Amendment abolishing slavery and was instrumental in securing its passage. Not long before she died, Elizabeth wrote in her diary that she had been unfair to Lincoln:

I see now the wisdom of his course, leading public opinion slowly but surely up to the final blow for freedom. ... My conscience pricks me now when I recall how I worked and prayed in 1864 for [his] defeat.... So when his birthday comes round each year I celebrate it somewhat in sackcloth and ashes.[38]

April 1865: that glorious and tragic month brought both the end of the Civil War and the assassination of Abraham Lincoln. Soon the women's movement was to face a new threat. The truth of Elizabeth's words would become even more apparent: "So long as woman labors

73

to second man's endeavors and exalt his sex above her own, her virtues pass unquestioned; but when she dares to demand rights and privileges for herself, her motives, manners, dress, personal appearance, and character are subjects for riducule and detraction."

The slaves were free; Congress now set about to determine their political status. In doing so they were to write the word "male" into the Constitution of the United States for the first time. The social reformer Robert Dale Owen, of Indiana, sent to the Woman's Loyal League copies of the various bills presented in Congress and revealed some of the discussion about them. One congressman had proposed the word "persons" instead of "males."

"That will never do," came the objection. "That would enfranchise wenches."

"Suffrage for black men will be all the strain the Republican party can stand," another said. Indeed, that fear seemed to be the overriding one.

The ensuing battle split the women's movement. Wendell Phillips, now leading a national effort to gain citizenship for blacks, wrote to Elizabeth that trying to combine the two efforts would lose for the blacks more than women would gain. She wrote back, "May I ask in reply to your fallacious letter just one question based on the apparent opposition in which you place the Negro and woman. My question is this: Do you believe the African race is composed entirely of males?[39]

William Lloyd Garrison supported the women. He wrote to Elizabeth in April 1866,

I shall assuredly give my warm approval of your movement for impartial suffrage, without regard to sex; and record my protest against the proposed contitutional amendment, limiting

74

the ballot to males.

On the back of his letter Elizabeth wrote, "Bless the good man."[40] Frederick Douglass told her, "I have made up my mind that if you can forgive me for being a Negro, I can not do less than to forgive you for being a woman."

Elizabeth wrote to Susan B. Anthony, who was then in Kansas visiting her brother, "Come home and help!" The two sent letters to women throughout the country, explaining the crisis and enclosing petitions:

> To the Senate and House of Representatives: The undersigned women of the United States, respectfully ask an amendment to the Constitution that shall prohibit the several states from disenfranchising any of their citizens on the ground of sex.

Many abolitionists refused to sign the petition. "This is the Negro's hour" was the standard reply. Angrily, Elizabeth and Susan reminded their former co-workers that half of the Negro race was female. They turned to the Democrats for support; the Democrats were willing to help only to the extent that they could embarrass the Republicans. Susan and Elizabeth determined to call another convention to rouse women to work for their rights.

The first Woman's Rights Convention following the Civil War met in the Church of the Puritans in New York City on May 10, 1866. Theodore Tilton, editor of the *Independent*, and the Reverend Henry Ward Beecher spoke eloquently on behalf of woman suffrage. Then Susan presented a resolution that was unanimously adopted: the organization thereafter would demand universal suffrage and be known as the American Equal Rights Association. James Mott, Stephen S. Foster, and

Parker Pillsbury were among other men present who favored including both women and blacks in the suffrage campaign.

Fortunately, Elizabeth was at last free for her work. Her children were growing up: Daniel had graduated from college and was employed; Henry and Gerrit were starting out in law practice; Theodore was a student at Cornell; the girls, Margaret and Harriot, were approaching college age. Amelia Willard continued to care for the house and young Robert in her usual capable way, and Elizabeth now had no baby to demand her constant attention. Though the law forbade her to vote, there was nothing that prevented a woman from seeking office. Could a woman perhaps attract some attention and support through a political campaign?

Elizabeth was the first woman to try such a step. Using as her platform "free speech, free press, free men, and free trade," Elizabeth Cady Stanton filed for election to the United States Congress. Unable to give wholehearted support to either major party, she declared herself an independent. Several newspapers did treat her campaign in a dignified manner, arguing that such an able woman would be an asset to Congress. Finally, she received only twenty-four votes. Yet she was pleased with the discussion her action had evoked. In fact, present response was hardly comparable with the furor she had caused in 1848 at Seneca Falls.

At its convention in 1867 the American Equal Rights Association proved to be still divided on the franchise issue. Many women, apparently, were willing to postpone their own rights until the black male had been enfranchised. One of the highlights of the meeting was a speech by the remarkable abolitionist, Sojourner Truth, who had once been a slave in New York.

76

We are now trying for liberty that requires no blood [she said] that women shall have their rights. . . . Now, I want it done very quick. . . . Now, if you want me to get out of the world, you had better get the women votin' soon. I shan't go till I can do that.[42]

A convention was called to amend the New York Constitution by eliminating the word "white" and extending the vote to all males. Realizing that they would not have another such opportunity for twenty years, Elizabeth and Susan quickly went into action to strike the word "male" from the constitution.

Their campaign cost them the support of Horace Greeley and his influential *Tribune*. He told Elizabeth and Susan,

This is a critical period for the Republican party and the life of the nation. The word "white" in our constitution at this hour has a significance which "male" has not. It would be wise and magnanimous to hold your claims, though just and imperative, I grant, in abeyance until the Negro is safe beyond peradventure, and your turn will come next. I conjure you to remember that this is "the Negro's hour," and your first duty now is to go through the state and plead his claims.

"Suppose," replied Elizabeth,

Horace Greeley, Henry J. Raymond, and James Gordon Bennett were disenfranchised: what would be thought of them, if before audiences and in leading editorials they placed the claims of others to the ballot, to be lifted above their own heads? No, no, this is the hour to press woman's claims; we have stood with the black man in the constitution over half a century, and it is fitting now that the constitutional door is open that we should enter with him into the political kingdom of equality.

77

"Well," Greeley threatened, "if you persevere in your present plan, you need depend on no further help from me or the *Tribune*."[43]

On June 27, 1867, Elizabeth and Susan were given a hearing before the convention committee considering the question of woman suffrage. Horace Greeley, the chairman, said to Elizabeth, "You will please remember that the bullet and ballot go together. If you vote, are you ready to fight?"

"Certainly," was Elizabeth's instant reply. "We are ready to fight, sir, just as you fought in the late war, by sending our substitutes."[44]

Twenty thousand New Yorkers signed the petitions for woman suffrage that were presented to the entire convention. When word got about that the report from Greeley's committee would be negative, Susan and Elizabeth plotted with George William Curtis to have his petition presented last, just before Greeley gave his report.

Curtis rose and cleared his throat. "Mr. President, I hold in my hand a petition from Mrs. Horace Greeley and three hundred other women citizens of Westchester, asking that the word 'male' be stricken from the constitution."

Laughter rolled from the galleries. Horace Greeley, red-faced, solemnly prepared to present his recommendations:

Your committee does not recommend an extension of the elective franchise to women. However defensible in theory, we are satisfied that public sentiment does not demand and would not sustain an innovation so revolutionary and sweeping, so openly at war with a distribution of duties and functions between the sexes as venerable and pervading as government

78

itself, and involving transformations so radical in social and domestic life.[45]

Some weeks later Elizabeth and Susan found themselves, along with Horace Greeley, at the home of Alice Cary. Elizabeth noticed him coming toward them. "Prepare for a storm," she whispered to Susan.

"Good evening, Mr. Greeley," they both said warmly, each extending a hand.

He ignored the politeness. "You two ladies are about the best maneuverers among the New York politicians. You tried to bother me at the convention, and I confess that you succeeded. The way Curtis presented Mary's petition showed me that you had prepared the plan." Turning toward Elizabeth, he spoke with even more irritation. "You are always so desirous in public to appear under your own rather than your husband's name. Why did you in this case substitute 'Mrs. Horace Greeley' for 'Mary Cheney Greeley,' which was really on the petition?"

"Because," Elizabeth answered, "I wanted all the world to know that it was the wife of Horace Greeley who protested against her husband's report."

"Well," he snapped, "I have given strict orders at the *Tribune* office that you and your cause are to be tabooed in the future. If it is necessary to mention your name, you will be referred to as 'Mrs. Henry B. Stanton.'"[46]

He stomped off. Elizabeth and Susan looked at each other. "Another enemy," said Elizabeth. "When will our male friends cease expecting us to play the game on their terms?"

CHAPTER EIGHT

After the Civil War, the woman's rights movement came to focus almost exclusively on suffrage. Only twenty years earlier, Elizabeth Cady Stanton had shocked almost everyone with her suggestion that women be allowed to vote. Now most women were coming to realize that petitions and requests were not enough: legislators, they believed, would listen only to those who had the power to reelect them. Woman suffrage became the primary issue of a continuing public debate, forcing discussion of all other rights demanded at Seneca Falls into the background.

In the autumn of 1867, the state of Kansas was to hold the first referendum in the United States on the question of woman suffrage. At the same time, Kansans would vote on whether to give the vote to black males. In the months preceding the referendum, Elizabeth was asked to speak throughout the state on behalf of woman suffrage, along with Susan B. Anthony, Lucy Stone, her husband, Henry Blackwell, and Olympia Brown. Escorted by former Governor Charles Robinson, Elizabeth spent two months traveling throughout Kansas in a carriage. They brought along leaflets to pass out to people as well as two suitcases, a pail for watering the horses, and a basket of apples and crackers. Elizabeth spoke at all hours of the day in all types of settings, from a large mill to a barn to unfinished schoolhouses.

Sometimes they lost their way along the unmarked trails. The governor complimented Elizabeth on her courage in very trying situations, yet at times she was quite anxious though she did not show it. Some days their diet consisted only of dried herring, crackers, slippery elm, and gum arabic; no milk or sugar for coffee, only sorghum. Elizabeth was repelled by bacon floating in grease and biscuits green with soda, but she said nothing. They slept in pioneer cabins wherever they could find people willing to spare a couple of mattresses. Once Elizabeth, to her horror, discovered mice in her bed. "What is that?" she asked, startled by a strange sound.

"Is your bed comfortable?" asked her host from the corner.

"Oh, yes," she answered, "but I thought I felt a mouse run over my head."

"Well," said the voice from the corner, "I should not wonder. I heard such squeaking from that corner during the past week that I told sister there must be a mouse nest in that bed."

Elizabeth was so tired she fell asleep in spite of the mouse. Her romantic notions about pioneer life rapidly disappeared. The unfinished houses, the people suffering from malaria, the children who had lost their mothers to the hardships of the journey—all convinced Elizabeth that something stronger than mere "Western fever" should motivate a man before he exposed his family to such a life. "There is no royal road to wealth and ease, even in the Western states!" she wrote. Coping with the difficulties of the trip, however, gave her renewed self-respect and the satisfaction of knowing that she could endure hardships without losing her sense of humor.

While the Republicans in Kansas were in favor of giving the vote to black males, Elizabeth and the other suffragists hoped to make the enfranchisement of women a nonpartisan issue and welcomed support from Democrats. Their efforts were heroic, but they received less than one-third of the votes cast. Black male suffrage did not succeed either. Elizabeth blamed the failure on the Republican policy of pitting one issue against the other. "A policy of injustice," she remarked, "always bears its own legitimate fruit in failure." Governor Robinson wrote to her after the election, "I thank you for all you have done for me and Kansas. Now we all love you as one of the chosen few who are to regenerate the world."[47]

George Francis Train, a wealthy eccentric who had also spoken on behalf of woman suffrage in Kansas, accompanied Elizabeth Cady Stanton and Susan B. Anthony back to New York. He offered to pay all expenses of the journey and of meetings in major cities along the way. Many of their friends were critical when Elizabeth and Susan accepted the offer. Aware of Train's eccentricities, of his standing as a Democrat, and of his reputation for being anti-Negro, Elizabeth defended their decision to take his money. "He is willing to devote energy and money to our cause," she wrote to Martha C. Wright,

> when no other man is. They might better turn their attention to Wendell Phillips, who by his false philosophy has paralyzed the very elect. To think of Boston women holding an antislavery festival when their own petitions are ignored in the Senate of the United States![48]

83

Elizabeth and Susan constantly marveled at the incapacity of their male friends—Phillips, William Lloyd Garrison, Frederick Douglass, Horace Greeley, and the popular and influential New York minister Henry Ward Beecher—to understand that women felt as keenly those injustices based on sex as black men did those based on color. Only Robert Purvis, a wealthy Philadelphia merchant, stood by them. Himself a black, he often declared the he would not want his son enfranchised unless his daughter could vote as well.

At this point the women realized that they needed a rostrum from which to promote their cause. Susan had long dreamed of publishing her own newspaper to demand not only the vote but all the other rights women were denied. The only thing they had lacked was financing, and now the money was found. When Elizabeth and Susan returned to New York, George Francis Train and another Democrat, David Melliss, provided the funds for them to set up their own newspaper, *The Revolution*. The first issue appeared January 6, 1868. Susan was publisher; Elizabeth Cady Stanton and Parker Pillsbury, formerly of the *Anti-Slavery Standard* and a staunch supporter of woman's rights, were the editors. For Elizabeth, the next two and one-half years were the happiest and most useful of her life.

The Revolution published opinions on all subjects that concerned the trio and refused to advertise anything in which they did not believe. When one of the staff included an advertisement for medicinal soda that displeased Elizabeth, she said so editorially in the next number. She was alone in the office one day soon after that when a man stormed in. "Who runs this concern?" he demanded.

"You will find the names of the editors and publishers on the editorial page," replied Elizabeth.

"Are you one of them?"

"I am."

"Well, do you know that I agreed to pay twenty dollars to have that advertised for one month, and then you condemn it editorially. Have you any more thoughts to publish on that medicine?"

"Oh, yes," answered Elizabeth, cheerfully. "I have not exhausted the subject yet."

"Then I will have the advertisement taken out," said the man. "What is there to pay for one insertion?"

"Oh, nothing, as the editorial probably did you more injury than the advertisement did you good."

As the man left, he remarked, "I prophesy a short life for this paper; the business world is based on quackery, and you cannot live without it."

"I fear you are right," said Elizabeth sadly.

At about the same time *The Revolution* started publication, Train went to England where his sympathies for the Irish people in their struggle against the English resulted in his spending a year in prison. Soon, in spite of financial help from David Melliss, the paper was in debt. The causes advocated by *The Revolution* were not popular, and the staff refused shady advertising. Train, realizing that he personally generated some of the unpopularity, insisted on severing all connections with the paper.

New friends joined Elizabeth and Susan in their efforts, all of them activists in the women's cause: Anna Dickinson, the nationally known young orator; Paulina Wright Davis, the wealthy former editor of *The Una*, who had gained some notoriety for using a manikin to illustrate her lectures in elementary physiology; Matilda

85

Joslyn Gage of upstate New York, a scholar who would later assist Elizabeth and Susan in writing the *History of Woman Suffrage*. Elizabeth B. Phelps bought a large house at 49 East Twenty-third Street and called it the Women's Bureau; she invited *The Revolution* to occupy the first floor and helped the paper to stay alive for a while longer.

Yet another factor led to the journal's demise. The Fourteenth Amendment, ratified July 28, 1868, made black men citizens and excluded women.

> All persons born or naturalized in the United States . . . are citizens of the United States. . . . When the right to vote at any election is denied to any of the *male* inhabitants of each state . . . the basis of representation therein shall be reduced in the proportion which the number of such *male* citizens shall bear to the whole number of *male* citizens . . . in such state. [Italics added.]

Since the amendment was not strong enough to guarantee suffrage for black males in some states, the supporters of black male suffrage pushed through a Fifteenth Amendment. Elizabeth and Susan were among those determined that the Fifteenth Amendment would include women. From *The Revolution* office they sent peitions all over the country for people to sign and forward to Congress. But the very same women who had been praised for their efforts to collect emancipation petitions were now called selfish and unreasonable. The Republicans branded them "Copperheads"[49] because they were supported by the Democratic Party, which was trying to win friends as it sought to rebuild itself after the Civil War.

To Elizabeth's great dismay, even her cousin Gerrit

Smith refused to sign the women's petition. Elizabeth replied to him in *The Revolution*, January 14, 1869: "Tyranny on a Southern plantation is far more easily seen by white men in the North than the wrongs of the women in their own households."[50] To demonstrate the further hypocrisy of northern men, *The Revolution* pointed out that while these good gentlemen were trying to force black suffrage on the South, they were refusing to allow blacks the right to vote in Connecticut, Michigan, Minnesota, Ohio, and Pennsylvania.

Elizabeth was distressed that many women, conditioned to self-sacrifice, had once again put aside their own interests to work for those of men. She and Susan had, during the Civil War, learned the hard lesson that women must never stop fighting for their rights, for once they put the rights of any other group before their own, they themselves lose ground. When Lucy Stone disagreed with her old friends, supporting two separate amendments (one for blacks and one for women), Elizabeth reminded her of what had happened in Kansas, where proponents of woman suffrage were pitted against proponents of black suffrage, and both groups lost.

The Revolution opposed the passage of Amendment XV. Elizabeth wrote, on October 21, 1869, that it reflected "the old idea of woman's inferiority, her subject condition." Furthermore, men had no right to pass the amendment without the consent of women.[51] Nonetheless, the Fifteenth Amendment—enfranchising black males and again excluding women—was ratified, March 30, 1870. ("The right of citizens of the United States to vote shall not be denied or abridged by the United States or by any State on account of race, color, or previous condition of servitude.") When the women—who felt it would have been a simple matter to insert the word "sex" next to "race" and "color"—proposed a Sixteenth Amendment, the men who had urged them to work for the blacks and await their turn, failed to appear with the promised support. Another half century would pass before women received the right to vote and the forgotten half of the black race achieved political rights. On March 15, 1869, just a year before the final ratification of the Fifteenth Amendment, Representative George W. Julian of Indiana, urged by Elizabeth Cady Stanton and Susan B. Anthony, introduced to the Congress the new Sixteenth Amendment.

The Right of Suffrage in the United States shall be based on citizenship, and shall be regulated by Congress; and all citizens of the United States whether native or naturalized shall enjoy this right equally without any distinction or discrimination whatever founded on sex.

That May, as the Fifteenth Amendment was being debated, the Equal Rights Association held its annual convention in New York City. Attendance was quite large. Because the president, Lucretia Mott, was absent, Elizabeth took the chair. After the routine opening business, Stephen Foster rose and remarked that some of the officers nominated, particularly the presiding officer, had repudiated the principles of the society.

"I would like you to say in what respect," Elizabeth demanded.

"I will with pleasure," Foster replied, "for, ladies and gentlemen, I admire our talented president with all my heart, and love the woman." The audience laughed. "But I believe she had publicly repudiated the principles of the society."

Once more Elizabeth insisted, "I would like Mr. Foster to state in what way."

Foster replied that *The Revolution* stood for edu·cated, rather than universal suffrage. He hotly criticized George Francis Train. He cited Elizabeth's refusal to support Amendment XV. "If you choose to put officers here that ridicule the Negro, and pronounce the Amendment infamous, why I must retire; I can not work with you."[52]

Henry Blackwell, Lucy Stone's husband, rose to the defense of his old friend. He criticized some of Train's contributions to *The Revolution*, but he pointed out that Train had withdrawn from the paper. "You," he said, "who know the real opinions of Miss Anthony and Mrs. Stanton on the question of Negro suffrage, do not believe that they mean to create antagonism between the Negro and the woman question. If they did disbelieve in Negro suffrage, it would be no reason for excluding them. We should no more exclude a person from our platform for disbelieving Negro suffrage than a person should be excluded from the antislavery plat-form for disbelieving woman suffrage."

Frederick Douglass, after paying tribute to Elizabeth, repeated his conviction that the black man was in much greater need of the vote than woman. Susan leaped to her feet. "Mr. Douglass talks about the wrongs of the Negro," she said, "but with all the outrages that he today suffers, he would not exchange his sex and take the place of Elizabeth Cady Stanton!" The laughing audience applauded wildly.[53] Later in the meeting when Ernestine Rose moved that the group change its name from the Equal Rights Association to the Woman Suffrage Association, Lucy Stone announced that she would oppose such a move until the black man had the right to vote.

A split was developing within the group, and the issue of woman suffrage versus black male suffrage was only one of the issues. Some of the women accused Elizabeth Cady Stanton of advocating free love because she was so outspoken on the need for liberal divorce laws. Now that suffrage was at last a respectable matter for debate, the more conservative women wanted to avoid talking about controversial issues. Believing that further controversy would weaken their chance of winning the ballot, they opposed raising sensitive issues in *The Revolution.*

At the end of the formal convention, delegates from nineteen states met at the Women's Bureau to form the National Woman Suffrage Association (NWSA). Because of prior disputes with men in the Equal Rights Association, the women agreed to keep control of the group entirely in the hands of women. Men might join, but they could not hold office. Elizabeth Cady Stanton became the first president of the organization, which then turned its immediate efforts toward passage of a Sixteenth Amendment giving women the right to vote.

That autumn, the Boston group broke with the NWSA and formed the American Woman Suffrage Association. Not only was there dissent over suffrage, there were personal disagreements as well. For years Susan B. Anthony and Lucy Stone had failed to get along with each other in spite of many efforts by Elizabeth to reconcile their differences. Remaining with Elizabeth and Susan in the National Association were Lucretia Mott, Martha C. Wright, Ernestine Rose, the Polish-born orator who was one of the first women to try to gain woman's rights through legislation, Paulina Wright Davis, the Reverend Olympia Brown (one of the earliest women ministers), Matilda Joslyn Gage, Anna E.

Dickinson, Elizabeth Smith Miller, Mary Cheney Greeley, and others.

The Revolution continued to lose money even though President Andrew Johnson and at least three United States Senators were among its subscribers, and even though Susan had spent ten thousand dollars of her own funds in the effort to maintain the journal. They had supported too many unpopular causes to hope for wide circulation. Moreover, their competitor, the more conservative *Woman's Journal*, published by the Boston faction, had attracted more subscribers. Since there was little demand for more than one women's publication, Susan finally conceded. On May 22, 1870, she sold the paper for one dollar to Laura Curtis Bullard, a New York writer. *The Revolution* was transformed into a literary and society paper. Eighteen months later it was bought by the New York *Christian Enquirer.*

"You and Parker Pillsbury gone and our *Revolution* no more!" Elizabeth sadly wrote to Susan. "And think of our sacred columns full of the advertisements of quack remedies!" She promised her friend that she would continue to write for the cause of women.[54] There was too much to do to become discouraged.

And by the end of 1870, women could see at least a little progress in the direction of winning suffrage. Wyoming and Utah had become the first of the territories to give female citizens the right to vote.

CHAPTER NINE

In 1869 Elizabeth Cady Stanton began speaking for the New York Lyceum Bureau, a job that, for the next twelve years, would take her on national tours from October until June. The lyceum circuit was quite popular in that day of no radio or television, and people in small towns and rural areas depended on such lectures for entertainment and cultural enlightenment. Managers kept ten percent of what the speakers earned, so it was to their advantage to book lecturers as frequently as possible. At times Elizabeth had to travel night and day, frequently arriving just in time to speak and be off once more as soon as she had finished. Her itinerary had been carefully prepared, but trains were off schedule more often than not.

She enjoyed meeting other speakers on the tour— Anna Dickinson, Frederick Douglass, Wendell Phillips, Theodore Tilton. Sometimes on Sundays they would relax together in a comfortable hotel. She missed her family. However, capable Amelia Willard was still supervising the Stanton home, and Elizabeth's lecture fees helped pay many of her children's college expenses. Henry B. Stanton was a respected writer and lawyer, but he was not rich; seven children often strained the family income.

On the lyceum circuit Elizabeth endured more than

the state of Iowa," mocked Elizabeth. When she described her experiences, the men were astonished and abashed. All of the lecture bureaus reported that their women speakers met their engagements more punctually than their men and bore the strain of travel in better humor.

During her travels, Elizabeth especially enjoyed talking with women, and she heartily approved of the less formal style in which western women lived. She opened windows in every train she rode, seeking to educate her fellow passengers to the advantages of fresh air. She continued her crusade to educate young mothers on the proper care of their babies: no hoods or woolen caps indoors, no swaddling bands, but always water to drink when they fussed. In order to draw women's attention to correct practices of infant care, she lectured on "Marriage and Maternity." Other popular lecture topics were "Our Girls," "Our Boys," "Prison Life," "Coeducation," and "Marriage and Divorce." On the topic of "Our Girls," one of her best-received talks, Elizabeth urged that girls be allowed to develop freely and independently without being forced into a mold. She thought of her own independent daughters, of the time when Henry had come home and found Harriot high in the chestnut tree in their yard.

"My daughter, come down, come down, you will fall," he called out, obviously agitated.

Poised calmly on the branch, Harriot replied, "Why don't you tell Bob to come down?" she demanded. "He's three years younger and one branch higher!"[55]

Elizabeth and Henry later chuckled about the scene. Both of them were proud of their spirited, adventuresome daughters.

During the summer of 1871, Elizabeth Cady Stanton

long hours and unpalatable coffee. Once she was scheduled to speak in Maquoketa, Iowa. At noon she arrived in a small town along the way, only to learn that the trains were not running any farther because of snow.

"Well," she said to the hotel owner, "I must be at Maquoketa at eight o'clock tonight; have you a sleigh, a span of horses, and a skillful driver? If so, I will go across the country."

"Oh, yes, madam," replied the man, "I have all that you ask; but you could not stand a six hours' drive in this piercing wind."

Elizabeth was used to the cold of New York winters. "Get the sleigh ready," she told him, "and I will try it."

After sending word by telegraph that she was on her way, she bundled up for the journey. The motel owner threw a large buffalo robe over the carriage. "There," he said. "If you can only sit perfectly still, you will come out all right at Maquoketa; that is, if you get there, which I very much doubt."

After an arduous drive against the wind and through drifts, Elizabeth arrived at her destination promptly at eight o'clock. She learned that all the roads in northern Iowa were blocked, so she continued her travels, forty to fifty miles per day, by sleigh. In Chicago three weeks later, she met Charles Bradlaugh and General Kilpatrick, who were supposed to have been traveling the same route just ahead of her.

"Well," smiled Elizabeth, "where have you gentlemen been?"

"Waiting here for the roads to be opened. We have lost three weeks' engagements," they answered.

"General, since you are lecturing on your experiences in Sherman's march to the sea, I can not understand how you are unable, in an emergency, to march across

95

and Susan B. Anthony traveled from New York to San Francisco, holding suffrage meetings in major cities en route. They enjoyed the variety of the scenery and their encounters with many women on their trip. Elizabeth sometimes spoke in Methodist churches and always praised that denomination for removing the word "obey" from the marriage service. "I think," she commented, "all these reverend gentlemen who insist on the word 'obey' in the marriage service should be removed for a clear violation of the Thirteenth Amendment to the Federal Constitution, which says there shall be neither slavery nor involuntary servitude within the United States." She attacked the Episcopal marriage service for its "humiliating ceremony" of giving the bride away. It represented, she believed, the transfer of a young woman from one master (her father) to another (her husband).

Elizabeth was in Nebraska when, in 1875, a constitutional convention was meeting in Lincoln. An amendment had been introduced to omit the word "male" from the document. Elizabeth had a suitcase full of Representative Benjamin Butler's minority reports from the Judiciary Committee of the United States House of Representatives, favoring woman's right to vote. While it was being loaded onto the boat, that suitcase fell into the Platte River, but fortunately, it was recovered. Elizabeth was escorted to the governor's house when she reached Lincoln; there she spread the valuable papers out in the sunshine to dry.

Elizabeth, who had addressed the convention, spent time afterwards discussing her speech with delegates. At one point a very small man tried to be witty at her expense, moved up his chair, seated himself directly facing her, and asked, "Don't you think that the best thing a woman can do is to perform well her part in the role of wife and mother? My wife has presented me with eight beautiful children; is not this a better life-work than that of exercising the right of suffrage?"

Sensing that the other men disapproved of his disrespectful attitude, Elizabeth looked the man over from head to foot. Then she answered, "I have met few men in my life worth repeating eight times."

The others roared with laughter. One of them said, "There, sonny, you have read and spelled; you better go." All the Nebraska papers published an account of the incident. The unfortunate man was asked everywhere he went, "Why doesn't Mrs. Stanton think you are worth repeating eight times?"

While in Lincoln, Elizabeth attended a celebration for the opening of a new railroad. In their speeches, the men congratulated themselves on the progress their state had made since it was organized as a territory in 1854. One man said, "This state was settled by three brothers, John, James, and Joseph, and from them have sprung the great concourse of people that greet us here today." Elizabeth turned to the governor. "Did all these people spring from the brains of John, James, and Joseph?" she asked. At the governor's urging, she asked that question of the speaker when he paused for breath. The crowd cheered. After that the speakers paid proper tribute to the women of Nebraska.

Eighteen seventy-three marked the twenty-fifth anniversary of the Seneca Falls convention. In the midst of her many activities, Elizabeth paused to take stock of those years. The demands of Seneca Falls were still not realized, but some of them, at least, were no longer subjects publicly ridiculed. Once the issues had been raised, repeated debate and discussion had served to

97

make them more acceptable to a growing number of people. Having survived the bloomer outfit, the setbacks of the Civil War, the failure to include women in two constitutional amendments, and much public criticism, the movement was still growing.

Women were rapidly becoming conscious of their rights and their needs. Isolated local groups had spread across the country, and gains were especially obvious in the less tradition-bound atmosphere of the western states. There were now two "national" suffrage organizations although Elizabeth deplored the split and believed that lack of unity harmed their common cause.

She remained firmly convinced that suffrage, crucial though it was, must not be the only goal for which women worked. After all, it was merely a tool of use in acquiring other rights: that is, social, political, legal, and economic equality. This belief had already caused disagreements with conservative women and would cause even more in the future. But Elizabeth thrived on challenges. Not for one minute did she regret those bold steps in 1848.

Women were learning that they must do their own work and promote their own causes rather than depend on men to do things for them. That spirit of independence was leading women to break into professions previously closed to them: medicine, law, the ministry, science. Although the movement was almost entirely a middle-class and upper-middle-class phenomenon during this period, working women were also striving for improvement in their lives and work. A few women were organizing and agitating for better conditions in factories and shops. *The Revolution*, during its short life, had frequently urged reforms to benefit working women.

Another anniversary quickly followed in 1876: the centennial of the United States of America! People all over the country were excited about festivities and exhibitions in Philadelphia. From coast to coast letters poured in to Elizabeth, who was serving as president of the National Woman Suffrage Association, demanding that a Woman's Declaration of Rights be issued in Philadelphia on July 4. Susan requested of General Joseph R. Hawley, president of the centennial commission, seats for fifty women at the celebration in Independence Hall, but was told there was no room. She then got a reporter's pass as a representative of her brother's newspaper, the Leavenworth *Times*. Later Elizabeth, Lucretia Mott, Sara Andrews Spencer, and Matilda Joslyn Gage received invitations.

Elizabeth wrote to General Hawley requesting the chance to present the Woman's Declaration of Rights after the reading of the Declaration of Independence. "We do not ask to read our declaration, only to present it to the president of the United States, that it may become an historical part of the proceedings."[56] She was turned down, ostensibly because the program had already been planned.

Elizabeth and Lucretia Mott decided not to accept the seats they had been offered but to hold a woman's convention simultaneously in the First Unitarian Church. Active workers for women's causes on both state and national levels, Susan B. Anthony, Matilda Joslyn Gage, Sara Andrews Spencer, Lillie Devereux Blake, and Phoebe W. Couzins agreed to use the press passes to attend the official festivities. In the oppressive heat of the day they took their Declaration to the ceremonies. When Richard Henry Lee of Virginia finished reading the Declaration of Independence, they stood up and walked down the aisle. Susan made a brief speech as she presented their document to the presiding officer, who turned pale as he accepted it. On their way out the women passed copies through the audience. Meanwhile, General Hawley on the platform, shouted, "Order! order!" Once they were outside the building, the women used the platform intended for the musicians in front of Independence Hall. Susan read the Woman's Declaration of Rights to an approving crowd as Matilda Joslyn Gage shielded her from the sun with an umbrella.

Then the five women hurried off to report to the convention Elizabeth had called at the Unitarian Church. Everyone was excited to hear of the morning's events, and Elizabeth chuckled as Susan described the expression on General Hawley's face.

Later, reflecting on that historic day, she noted that most people then could not understand why women would choose to complain of injustice on so joyous an occasion, especially when most American women seemed to be quite happy. "The history of the world shows," she mused, "that the vast majority, in every generation, passively accept the conditions into which they are born, while those who demand larger liberties are ever a small, ostracized minority, whose claims are ridiculed and ignored."

The National Woman Suffrage Association convention of January 1877 marked another turning point in the woman's rights movement. Defeated in two Constitutional amendments (XIV and XV) and in test cases in the courts, the women decided to devote their energies to securing a new amendment. Annual meetings in Washington, D.C., helped maintain constant pressure on Congress. The rival American Woman Suffrage Association, rather than concentrating its efforts on one Constitutional amendment, turned toward action on the state level. The National Association persisted; it was the amendment drafted by Elizabeth Cady Stanton, reintroduced year after year, which was finally passed in 1919. By then the younger suffragists, wishing to honor Susan B. Anthony for her work in the cause, named the amendment the "Susan B. Anthony Amendment." But the original had come from the pen of Elizabeth Cady Stanton.[57]

During one of the Washington conventions, Isabella Beecher Hooker held a prayer meeting in the women's reception room next to the Senate chamber. Elizabeth reported to Susan, "I did not attend the prayer meeting, for, as Jehovah has never taken a very active part in the suffrage movement, I thought I would stay at home and get ready to implore the committee, having more faith in their power to render us the desired aid."[58]

Along with her work for the National Woman Suffrage Association, Elizabeth had maintained her tiring pace on the lecture circuit. Her fees had helped send Margaret and Harriot to Vassar College, and Theodore and Robert to Cornell. Theodore had also earned a master's degree and had gone abroad to study and work as a foreign correspondent for the New York *Tribune*. In the fall of 1880, tired of traveling eight months a year, Elizabeth retired from the circuit.

Since Henry was now a successful writer for the New York *Sun*, he and Elizabeth could relax somewhat. They thoroughly enjoyed visits from friends and children at their home in Tenafly, New Jersey. But most of all they cherished their moments alone together—the evening walks and carriage rides by moonlight. They took pleasure in long discussions about their current interests as well as remembrances of their earlier years.

On November 12, 1880, Elizabeth Cady Stanton celebrated her sixty-fifth birthday. To Harriot and Theodore she wrote, "Looking back through life, I feel that our troubles are fully compensated by our joys. I have had an existence of hard work, but I think it has been a success." In the same letter, she told them about the recent election day when she had actually tried to vote.

CHAPTER TEN

A new militancy had arisen among women toward the end of the century. When Amendments XIV and XV had failed to grant females the right to vote, about one hundred fifty women throughout the country voted or else tried to do so. Marilla M. Ricker, of New Hampshire, was the first, in 1870. Susan B. Anthony and several other Rochester women had voted in the 1872 presidential election and had been arrested for their efforts. When the case came to trial in June 1873, the presiding judge refused to allow the case to be heard before a jury and fined Susan one hundred dollars. A technicality prevented her from taking the case to the United States Supreme Court, as she had wanted to do, but she never paid the fine. Virginia Minor, of St. Louis, lost a court battle to win the right to vote. Some women refused to pay taxes where they were denied the franchise.

On November 2, 1880, Elizabeth wrote her children, the Republican wagon and horses, decorated with flags, came by to take the male members of the Stanton household to the polls.

"My legal representative is absent, but I will go down and vote," Elizabeth told the driver.

"You flabbergast me," he replied.

But Elizabeth was determined to give a practical

demonstration of the cause for which she had worked so long. "I'll take the risk and go down with you, notwithstanding your condition," she insisted.

Once at the polls, Elizabeth had to convince the "old Dutch inspectors" that she was indeed qualified to vote. After all, she was well past twenty-one, and she had lived in Tenafly for twelve years. She paid her taxes, she owned property, and she could read and write. The inspectors refused to allow her to place her ballot in the box. By this time a crowd had gathered. Finally she flung her ballot toward the box and left. "The whole town is agape with my act," she wrote. "A friend says he never saw Tenafly in such excitement." The next evening she went to the post office for the mail. Said the postmaster, "I would give five dollars for your ballot. I would have it framed and hung up in my home."[59]

On her sixty-fifth birthday Elizabeth Cady Stanton also began the diary she was to keep for the rest of her life. She reminisced in the first entry:

Once in a while, in thinking of what I might have done for my children, I feel suddenly depressed. But as I did not see, when I myself was young, all that I now see with age and experience, I dismiss the thoughts from my mind with the reflection that I then knew no better than to have seven children in quick succession.[60]

The very next day Elizabeth was deeply saddened to read in the *Tribune* that her beloved friend, Lucretia Mott, was dead. "I have vowed again," she wrote, "as I have many times, that I shall in the future try to imitate her noble example."[61]

Elizabeth looked to the past during her birthday.

reflections, but much of her greatest work—as a writer—was yet to come. Matilda Joslyn Gage and Susan B. Anthony had arrived in Tenafly to begin with her a task they had been discussing for several years. They had been busy for months collecting materials for the *History of Woman Suffrage*. Elizabeth had never dreamed how many details must be considered in writing history. As they stood before piles of material which increased with every mail delivery, she exclaimed, "I feel as if our lifework still lies before us!"

For weeks they sorted and compiled, often working until midnight. Many letters and clippings set the three women to talking about some amusing or controversial incident from the past. They had planned to publish a pamphlet, but they greatly underestimated their task. Sometimes there were disagreements: Elizabeth and Susan clung to opposing points of view, only to resolve their conflicts after a break for relaxation. By Christmas time, when Matilda Joslyn Gage returned home, Elizabeth was still thankful to be writing rather than making "those weary lecture tours."

Volume I of the *History of Woman Suffrage*, which covered the years from 1848 to 1861, was published in May 1881. "I welcomed it with the same feeling of love and tenderness as I did my firstborn," Elizabeth wrote. "I took the same pleasure in hearing it praised, and felt the same mortification in hearing it criticized." Susan had to assume major financial responsibility to secure the publication by Fowler and Wells.

The first of June, 1881, found Elizabeth at work on the second volume of the History. She and Susan busied themselves in a large, sunny room with a bay window and a library table. Almost buried in manuscripts, old newspapers, and reams of yellow writing paper, they

105

paused occasionally to admire the bright nasturtiums in the center of the table or munch on a pear or a few grapes which Elizabeth Smith Miller had sent. After a walk out-of-doors at noon, Elizabeth always took a nap before their two o'clock lunch hour. Then, back at the task before them, the two women continued to sort, compile, squabble, and laugh as the number of pages increased.[62]

Susan, who had taken a much-needed vacation, returned to Tenafly in late October. They worked on the *History* throughout the winter until Harriot returned from Europe in February and informed her mother that she was taking her back to England with her. Harriot wrote the long chapter on the American Woman Suffrage Association (which neither Susan nor Elizabeth wished to write) and read proof so that they could depart for France all the sooner. Finally Volume II of the *History of Woman Suffrage* was completed, and Elizabeth sighed with relief. The work was not yet finished, but the next volume would wait during the year and a half that Elizabeth spent in Europe.

On May 22, 1882, Elizabeth and Harriot sailed for France where Elizabeth became better acquainted with her son Theodore, his wife, Marguerite Berry, and their daughter, Elizabeth Cady Stanton. Harriot was studying at the university in Toulouse. Theodore was editing a book, *The Woman Question in Europe*, a series of essays about women in various European countries. He himself wrote the essay on France; all the others were written by women. Elizabeth spent much of her time helping Theodore polish the English translations of those essays.

In the fall, Elizabeth accompanied Harriot to England for her marriage to William H. Blatch. When Susan B. Anthony arrived, the two friends found themselves in a whirl of social events, receptions, and reform meetings.

On Sunday, May 20, 1883, Elizabeth preached in a Methodist Church in Bristol. She used as her text Genesis 1:27-28:

> So God created man in his own image, in the image of God he created him; male and female he created them. And God blessed them, and God said to them, "Be fruitful and multiply, and fill the earth and subdue it; and have dominion over the fish of the sea and over the birds of the air and over every living thing that moves upon the earth." (RSV)

More than ever, Elizabeth was finding religion a fascinating topic for thought, reading, and discussion. She was still attempting to put into perspective her childhood fears and dissatisfactions and to formulate beliefs that were meaningful and intellectually valid. Because religion was so important to most women and because so many women gave large amounts of time and energy to the church, she was especially concerned with what organized religion said about the image of woman.

Elizabeth was not afraid to express her views about sex, a subject which women of the Victorian Age were not even supposed to think about. After reading *Leaves of Grass*, she commented,

> Walt Whitman seems to understand everything in nature but women. In "There Is a Woman Waiting for Me," he speaks as if the female must be forced to the creative act, apparently ignorant of the great natural fact that a healthy woman has as much passion as a man, that she needs nothing stronger than the law of attraction to draw her to the male.[63]

In her awareness of women's sexual capacity, she had gone far beyond the thinking of her times.

Refreshed and stimulated by her European visit, Elizabeth was ready to return home and start work on Volume III of the *History of Woman Suffrage*. She was filled with new ideas that were just waiting to be written down. When Susan came to Johnstown with more boxes of documents, Elizabeth found it even more difficult than before to work with old instead of new material. She wanted to continue to write original articles for magazines. In December 1882, *North American Review* had published her article on "The Health of American Women," and she had just completed a piece for the same journal on "The Need of Liberal Divorce Laws" in which she insisted that there be no further legislation on the subject until women could take part in making the laws. The Johnstown *Democrat* ran a series of her articles about how untidy the local streets were; she urged passage of a law against throwing trash on the pavement.

Susan, the activist, was also restless. Yet both turned their attention to the *History* with their former discipline. Elizabeth read for an hour or two each night after Susan had gone to bed. For weeks they worked, and then they put aside the boxes of manuscripts until July 1885.

At this point Elizabeth had to go to Tenafly to tend to the repairing of the house they had rented out for the past three years. Upon her return two months later, back came Susan, and the work began afresh. "Oh, what dreadful manuscripts some women do send us!" Elizabeth exclaimed to her friend. "It is enough to destroy our old eyes."[64]

Finally, as the year ended, they completed Volume III; it was published in 1886. The *History of Woman Suffrage* had been brought up to date, but the story continued. Susan B. Anthony and Ida Husted Harper later wrote the fourth volume with advice and suggestions from Elizabeth. Later still, after she and Susan had died, Ida Harper would write the last two volumes of the monumental record of those long years of struggle. Susan used the money she received from the will of Eliza Jackson Eddy, of Boston, to distribute the *History* free of charge to public libraries throughout the country.[65]

CHAPTER ELEVEN

Religion, in the opinion of Elizabeth Cady Stanton, played so important a part in the lives of women that discrimination by the church could no longer be tolerated. During the last two decades of her life she conducted a vigorous and concentrated attack on all forms of bias against women by organized religion.

From 1888 on, goals other than suffrage concerned her increasingly as she continued her writing, sharply criticizing unjust divorce laws and inequality in organized religion. In that eventful year and those to come, her audience of readers grew, and as it did, the opposition from many younger, more conservative feminists became more pronounced.

For the most part, these were rather well-to-do young professional women who wanted, above all, to be "respectable." They were not lacking for money, and their social views were often narrow. (A notable exception was Dr. Anna Howard Shaw, whose early struggles as a physician in Boston slums helped her to relate to poor people.) Most of Elizabeth's younger critics were unwilling to risk losing converts to the cause of suffrage, and the last thing they wished to see was controversy on such "side issues" as divorce, trade unionism, and religion.

Yet Elizabeth, as well as Susan B. Anthony (now

spending much time with working women) and other veterans in the movement, was willing to collaborate with anyone who supported woman's rights, whatever her or his views on other subjects. And Elizabeth's talent as a writer, her ability to reason and present arguments effectively, stimulated thought and discussion even among those who disagreed with her. In time, many of her ideas that were rejected by these women would be accepted by feminists as self-evident truths. (In 1920, for example, after the Nineteenth Amendment had finally passed, women began to realize they were not any better off than before, and some concluded that Elizabeth Cady Stanton had represented the voice of reason in advising women to attack on other fronts of injustice.)

In May of 1888, in the *North American Review*, Elizabeth published an article entitled "Has Christianity Benefited Woman?" In it, she wrote:

> A consideration of woman's position before Christianity, under Christianity, and at the present time shows that she is not indebted to any form of religion for one step of progress, nor one new liberty; on the contrary, it has been through the perversion of her religious sentiments that she has been so long held in a condition of slavery.

The scholarly article revealed her thorough knowledge of history, literature, and civil and canon law. History proved to her that the "moral degradation of women" resulted more from "theological superstitions" than from all other causes put together. Citing woman's exalted position in ancient Egypt and honors and rights accorded women under Roman law and in the Germanic tribes, she contrasted these with the Apostle Paul's

112

attitude toward marriage, the polygamy of some of the early Christians and the Mormons, and the general degradation of women in Christian countries.

She accused the church of intellectual suppression, contending that it

> sedulously tried to keep all learning within itself. Man, seeking after knowledge, was opposed by the church; woman, by both church and man. Educated men in our own day, who have outgrown many of the popular theological superstitions, do not share with the women of their households the freedom they themselves enjoy.

There would not be any change until "another revision of the Protestant Bible shall strike from its pages all invidious distinctions based on sex." Gains were being made in almost all other walks of life, but most of the churches would not ordain women to the ministry, allow them to preach, or even, in some cases, to sing in the choirs. Therefore, Elizabeth concluded, "not until [women] make an organized resistance against the withering influences of canon law, will they rid themselves of the moral disabilities growing out of the theologies of our times."[66]

Elizabeth continued to find it ironic that the Christian churches, which taught the sacredness of the individual, should advocate the subjection of woman. It was not Jesus or his teachings that she found odious, but rather the interpretation of those teachings by various denominations and their theologies. Lamenting that the Bible was used to support many reactionary or conservative ideas, she wrote,

> When those who are opposed to all reforms can find no other argument, their last resort is the Bible. It has been interpreted

113

to favor intemperance, slavery, capital punishment, and the subjection of women.[67]

In January 1885, when the National Woman Suffrage Association convention was held in Washington, D.C., Elizabeth was presiding. She introduced a controversial resolution prepared by a committee of women and drafted by Clara Bewick Colby:

WHEREAS, The dogmas incorporated in religious creeds derived from Judaism, teaching that woman was an afterthought in the creation, her sex a misfortune, marriage a condition of subordination, and maternity a curse, are contrary to the law of God (as revealed in nature), and to the precepts of Christ, and,

WHEREAS, These dogmas are an insidious poison, sapping the vitality of our civilization, blighting woman, and, through her, paralyzing humanity; therefore be it

RESOLVED, That we call on the Christian ministry, as leaders of thought, to teach and enforce the fundamental idea of creation, that man was made in the image of God, male and female, and given equal rights over the earth, but none over each other. And, furthermore, we ask their recognition of the scriptural declaration that, in the Christian religion, there is neither male nor female, bond nor free, but all are one in Christ Jesus.[68]

A vehement discussion followed. Susan B. Anthony said, "I found long ago that this matter of settling any question of human rights by people's interpretation of the Bible is never satisfactory. I hope we shall not go back to that war. No two can ever interpret alike, and discussion upon it is wasted."[69]

Some of the delegates expressed fear of doing

anything to antagonize the churches, which were now beginning to support woman suffrage for the first time. Elizabeth was insistent. "You may go all over the world," she told the delegation, "and you will find that every form of religion which has breathed upon this earth has degraded women." She mentioned Hindu widows who burned themselves alive on the funeral pyres of their late husbands, Turkish women in harems, the Mormon practice of polygamy. "Man, of himself, could not do this; but when he declares, 'Thus saith the Lord,' of course he can do it." The churches of America, she continued, could not survive if it were not for the work women were doing, and yet what woman received the credit she deserved? "Have we ever yet heard a man preach a sermon from Genesis 1:27-28, which declares the full equality of the feminine and masculine element in the Godhead? They invariably shy at that first chapter. They always get up in their pulpits and read the second chapter."[70]

In the end Susan's point of view prevailed: the delegates voted to table the resolution. The text of the resolution, however, was printed in many newspapers and evoked much public disfavor. Elizabeth Cady Stanton was dissuaded no more easily than she had been in 1848. She had disagreed with Susan and with many other people before; she would continue to press her views, bluntly and fearlessly. As always, she was supremely confident of the logic of her position. She believed that anyone who reasoned the issues through would come to the same conclusion.

On November 12, 1885, Elizabeth's seventieth birthday, people from all over the country and the world paid her tribute. She was widely admired and loved, even by those who could not always agree with her. In the same month, she was the subject of the entire issue of Elizabeth Boynton Harbert's magazine, *The New Era*. Deeply touched by the praise she had received, Elizabeth wrote thank-you notes to those, like Robert Collyer and Frederick Douglass, whose words meant much to her.

On the evening of her birthday, when many of her friends and co-workers gathered at the New York City home of Dr. Clemence Lozier to honor her, she talked to them about "The Pleasures of Old Age," drawing inspiration from Henry Wadsworth Longfellow's *"Morituri Salutamus."* Fifty, not fifteen, is the heyday of a woman's life," she told them.

Then the forces hitherto finding an outlet in flirtations, courtship, conjugal and maternal love, are garnered in the brain to find expression in intellectual achievements, in spiritual friendships and beautiful thoughts, in music, poetry, and art. [She continued,] The young have no memories with which to guild their lives, none of the pleasures of retrospection. Neither has youth a monopoly of the illusions of hope, for that is eternal; to the end we have something still to hope. And here age has the advantage of basing its hopes on something rational and attainable. From experience we understand the situation, we have a knowledge of human nature, we learn how to control ourselves, to treat children with tenderness, servants with consideration, and our equals with proper respect. Years bring wisdom and charity; pity rather than criticism; sympathy, rather than condemnation.[71]

As her life continued to be rich and productive, Elizabeth was herself an example of her words.

Now that her part in the *History of Woman Suffrage* was complete, she had another project in mind. When Frances Lord, from London, visited her in Tenafly in

August 1886, Elizabeth presented an idea for a "woman's Bible." It would be an undertaking designed to correct the injustices to women contained in the Scriptures. Miss Lord was enthusiastic. The outline of the project was just beginning to take shape when Elizabeth sailed once more for England, on October 27, 1886. She spent the winter with Harriot and her family at Basingstoke, reading, writing, and continuing work on *The Woman's Bible.*

On January 12, 1887, Elizabeth was eating breakfast in her room when Harriot entered, her face pale. She handed her mother a cablegram from New York. Henry B. Stanton was dead.

"Death!" Elizabeth wrote in her diary that evening.

We all think we are prepared to hear of the passing away of the aged. But when the news comes, the heart and pulses all seem to stand still. We can not realize that those we have known in life are suddenly withdrawn, to be seen no more on earth. To be with them during their last sickness, to close their eyes, to look upon their lifeless form for the final days, and to go through the sad pageant that follows, helps one, little by little, to realize the change. But when the boundless ocean rolls between you and the lost one, and the startling news comes upon you without preparation, it is a terrible shock to every nerve and feeling, to body and mind alike. Then well up regrets for every unkind, ungracious word spoken, for every act of coldness and neglect. Ah! if we could only remember in life to be gentle and forebearing with each other, and to strive to serve nobly instead of exacting service, our memories of the past would be more pleasant and profitable. I have lived with my husband forty-six years, and now he leads the way to another sphere. What the next life is, whether this one is all, or we pursue an individual existence in a higher form of development, are the questions not yet answered.[72]

All day Elizabeth and Harriot sat and talked, considering the mysteries of life and death and discussing Henry B. Stanton. He had recently published a book, called *Random Recollections*. And on his eightieth birthday only a few short months before, he had been honored at a dinner by the New York City Press Club. Elizabeth remembered that occasion with pleasure, and she recalled, with tears in her eyes, her youthful pride in an abolitionist orator many years ago. She and Henry had been happy together in spite of long separations because they had respected each other so deeply. Each had been willing to allow the other complete individuality, and their love had been durable enough to last almost half a century.

Now, as always, Elizabeth did not allow herself to dwell on the past. Henry had been important for her, and she treasured the memories of those long years together, but life involved more than one person, even a beloved husband. Elizabeth observed about Tolstoy's *Anna Karenina*, "All the women are disappointed and unhappy. Well they may be, as they are made to look to men, and not to themselves, for their chief joy."[73] Unlike so many women, Elizabeth understood that it was best if husband and children were not the only focus of a woman's existence; that, especially when husband and children were gone, each woman needed her own interests and activities.

That spring she went to Paris where she spent six months, much of it getting to know her son Theodore better. Following his study of *The Woman Question in Europe*, he had published a second book. Elizabeth was proud to see her son interested in the ideas to which she had devoted her life. "To say that I have realized in him all I could desire, is the highest praise a fond mother can

118

give," she wrote.

To entertain friends and reformers in Paris, Elizabeth held Wednesday afternoon receptions. She frequently enjoyed concerts, operas, theater, and drives throughout the area, and on one occasion Monsieur Joseph Fabre escorted her to a reception at the Élysée Palace and presented her to President and Madame Jules Grevy. In contrast she found London rather drab when she returned in late October.

Back at Basingstoke once more, she felt carefree. "This is the first time in my life," she wrote in her diary,

> that I have had uninterrupted leisure for reading, free from all care of home, servants, and children. Mill, Richter, and Ruskin have been occupying my attention of late. What an impeachment of English wisdom and honesty the works of the last named![74]

The quiet was often broken by frequent invitations and visits from English suffragists and reformers. Then Susan ordered her to come home for the international convention they had planned for 1888. She sailed from Southampton on March 4.

The International Council of Women met in Washington, D.C., from March 25 through April 1, 1888. Contrasted to the hastily-convened and poorly-organized meeting at Seneca Falls in 1848, this meeting was elaborately conceived and organized, with the help of twelve thousand dollars. The National Woman Suffrage Association had voted the previous year to assume full responsibility for the gathering and had extended invitations to all women's associations in the trades, professions, and reforms. Fifty-three organizations were represented by eighty speakers and forty-nine delegates from the United States, Canada, England, Ireland, France, Norway, Finland, Denmark, and India. President and Mrs. Grover Cleveland were among those who received the delegates. There were suffrage hearings before both the House and the Senate. Reflecting on the events, Elizabeth wrote that such pressure on the Congress would someday be rewarded. "I do hope the departed can see what is going on on this earth, for I admit that such tardy recognition will give me pleasure even though I be enjoying the bliss of paradise."[75]

One result of the International Council of Women was a renewal of efforts to reunite the two suffrage associations. Alice Stone Blackwell and Rachel Foster Avery, secretaries of the two groups, prepared the plans for union. Elizabeth especially disapproved of the section of the proposed constitution that permitted men to hold office. "Think of an association of black men officered by slaveholders!" she wrote. "Having men pray or preside for us at our meetings has always seemed to me a tacit admission that we haven't the brains to do these things ourselves."[76] Her fears proved unnecessary, as most men soon retired from active roles in the new National American Woman Suffrage Association.

Another controversy arose over the presidency of the group. Most members of the old American Association thought Elizabeth was much too radical; they particularly opposed her outspoken views on religion and divorce and preferred Susan B. Anthony since Lucy Stone had flatly refused to serve in that office. Elizabeth won, although not unanimously, largely because Susan had vehemently urged the National members to vote for the woman who had served them so faithfully as president. Susan became vice-president-at-large; Lucy Stone was chairman of the executive committee.

Elizabeth was deeply honored as she made the opening address.

> For fifty years we have been plaintiffs in the courts of justice, but as the bench, the bar, and the jury are all men, we are nonsuited every time. Some men tell us we must be patient and persuasive; that we must be womanly. My friends, what is man's idea of womanliness? It is to have a manner which pleases him—quiet, deferential, submissive, approaching him as a subject does a master. He wants no self-assertion on our part, no defiance, no vehement arraignment of him as a robber and a criminal. What do we know yet of the womanly? The women we have seen thus far have been, with rare exceptions, the mere echoes of men. Man has spoken in the State, the Church and the Home, and made the codes, creeds and customs which govern every relation in life, and women have simply echoed all his thoughts and walked in paths he prescribed. And this they call womanly.

Even though she was aware that she might be offending some of the more conservative members of the old American Association, Elizabeth continued to talk of her favorite themes. Women must have equality in the churches. There should be no more laws regarding marriage and divorce until women have a part in making those laws. Next, she attacked the Women's Christian Temperance Union:

> As women are taking an active part in pressing on the consideration of Congress many narrow sectarian measures, such as more rigid Sunday laws (the stopping of travel and the distribution of mail on that day), and the introduction of the name of God into the Constitution; and as this action on the part of some women is used as an argument for the

disfranchisement of all, I hope this convention will declare that the Woman Suffrage Association is opposed to all union of Church and State, and pledges itself as far as possible to maintain the secular nature of our Government.

Speaking especially to the conservative element, she advocated a broad platform and free flow of ideas for the association. She welcomed all classes, races, and creeds of women. At the conclusion of her address, she proudly introduced her daughter, Harriot Stanton Blatch.[77] The audience gave them a standing ovation as they left the platform.

Just before the convention, Elizabeth had testified before the Senate Select Committee on Woman Suffrage. After her address, the chairman, Senator Zebulon B. Vance, of North Carolina, asked, "Would women be willing to go to war if they had the ballot?"

"We would decide first whether there would be war," answered Elizabeth.

You may be sure, Senator, that the influence of women will be against armed conflicts. Women will do their share of the work in the hospitals as elsewhere, and if they were enfranchised, the only difference would be—and it is an important one, Senator—that they would be paid for their services and pensioned at the close of the war.

Asked Senator Vance, "Would not women lose their refining influence and moral qualities if they engaged in man's work?"

"But," protested Elizabeth,

we must define what is "men's work." I find men in many avocations—washing, cooking, selling needles and tape over a counter—which might be considered the work of women. The consideration of questions of legislation, finance, free trade, etc., certainly would not degrade woman, nor is her refinement so evanescent a virtue that it could be swept away by some work which she might do with her hands. Queen Victoria looked as dignified and refined in opening Parliament as any lady I have ever seen.

Senator John Allen of Washington commented, "Your point is well made, Mrs. Stanton. But then you know I am in favor of woman suffrage."

Elizabeth smiled and turned to the committee chairman once more. "But, Senator Vance, may I ask how Mrs. Vance stands on the question?"

The Senator laughed. "Well, I suppose I must admit that I have got the worst of this discussion."[78]

Elizabeth repeated her address before the House Judiciary Committee. For the first time in history the committee issued a majority report favoring an amendment to the Constitution. As she sailed for England, Elizabeth was rightfully proud of her accomplishments. She had told the National American Woman Suffrage Association, "I consider it a greater honor to go to England as president of this association than would be the case if I were sent as minister plenipotentiary to any court in Europe."[79]

While Elizabeth was abroad word came that Wyoming had been admitted to the Union, the first state in which women could vote. "This triumph is enough for one year!" she wrote happily.[80]

Sad news came as well. While she was absent from home, Elizabeth learned of the death of her son Daniel and of her sister Tryphena. Turning to the future for consolation, she took charge of her granddaughters while Harriot Stanton Blatch and Marguerite Berry

Stanton visited London.

"Now," said Lizette, "we will have five days of peace; no lessons, no scales, no scolding."

"Yes," agreed Nora, "Queen Mother always says 'yes' to everything."[81] And so "Queen Mother" dressed dolls for them and amused them with her stories. Sadly, she left them and their parents when she returned home late in the summer of 1891, perhaps realizing that she would never again return to Europe. Still, she looked forward to a long visit with Susan at Rochester.

Susan, who had hoped that Elizabeth would now come to live with her, was deeply disappointed when she did not. Elizabeth's children would not permit her to go, and she herself preferred to remain in New York.

When her son-in-law died, her daughter Margaret, her son Robert, and she rented an apartment at 26 East Sixty-first Street in New York City, and there she resumed the active life she had led before.

CHAPTER TWELVE

When the National American Woman Suffrage Association convened in Washington, D.C., in January 1892, Elizabeth, now seventy-six, insisted that she be allowed to retire from the presidency. Susan B. Anthony was elected to serve in her place, and the Reverend Dr. Anna Howard Shaw became vice-president-at-large. Elizabeth Cady Stanton and Lucy Stone were made honorary presidents. After forty years of active participation, this was Elizabeth's last appearance at a national convention, but she continued to send speeches for Susan to read to the organization, in order to make her views known. The following year Lucy Stone died. Of that magnificent trio that had led the suffrage movement, only Susan B. Anthony remained active. At that last convention, Elizabeth delivered what most people considered her greatest address, "The Solitude of Self." It was her personal credo derived from her long years of private life and public experience. She spoke of the "individuality of each human soul." The woman as an individual first has the right "to use all her faculties for her own safety and happiness." As a citizen, she should have the same rights as any other citizen. As a woman, she deserved "individual happiness and development." Only the "incidental relations of life"—mother, wife, daughter—may demand "special duties and training."

Such men as Herbert Spencer, she continued,

> uniformly subordinate her rights and duties as an individual, as
> a citizen, as a woman, to the necessities of these individual
> relations, some of which a large class of women never assume.
> In discussing the sphere of man we do not decide his rights as
> an individual, as a citizen, as a man, by his duties as a father, a
> husband, a brother or a son. . . .
>
> The isolation of every human soul [she told her audience]
> and the necessity of self-dependence must give each individual
> the right to choose his own surroundings. The strongest reason
> for giving woman all the opportunities for higher education,
> for the full development of her faculties, her forces of mind
> and body; for giving her the most enlarged freedom of thought
> and action; a complete emancipation from all forms of
> bondage, of custom, dependence, superstition; from all the
> crippling influences of fear—is the solitude and personal
> responsibility of her own individual life. The strongest reason
> we ask for woman a voice in the government under which she
> lives; in the religion she is asked to believe; equality in social
> life, where she is the chief factor; a place in the trades and
> professions, where she may earn her bread, is because of her
> birthright to self-sovereignty; because, as an individual, she
> must rely on herself.

In conclusion, she asked, "Who can take, dare take,
on himself, the rights, the duties, the responsibilities,
of another human soul?"[82]

Elizabeth repeated "The Solitude of Self" before the
Senate Committee on Woman Suffrage. She received so
many compliments that she confided to her diary that it
was the best piece she had ever written. As she was
leaving the Senate committee room, Senator Vance said
to her, "Well, Mrs. Stanton, the speeches of you ladies,
taken as a whole, surpass any I have ever heard on a
single subject, and their logic, if used in support of any

126

other measure, could not fail to carry it."

Shaking hands, Elizabeth rejoined, "Well, Senator, when you make your unfavorable minority report, for I suppose you are going to be guilty of such a political blunder, I mean to get out a special edition of it with a big *N. B.* at the end, followed with what you have just said."

"But that will kill the report," protested Senator Vance.

"Better kill the report than let it kill you."

"You ladies," he smiled wryly, "wish at least to be charitable to your enemies."[83] But Elizabeth, who charmed everyone with her twinkling blue eyes and grandmotherly manner, had no "enemies," merely friends who disagreed with her.

A few months later Elizabeth was honored at a luncheon given by the New York Woman Suffrage League. During the event her thoughts returned often to those difficult years in Seneca Falls. "Who would have believed then," she mused, "that in less than half a century, I, at that moment the laughingstock of the press and public, would today receive such a tribute in the very metropolis itself? Courage! What will not be the advance in another fifty years?"[84]

In 1895, Elizabeth Cady Stanton was eighty years old. Unknown to her, Susan had arranged to have the National Council of Women conduct the celebration on November 12. Newspapers throughout the nation, even those opposed to woman suffrage, honored her with features and editorials. Six thousand people from throughout the country filled the Metropolitan Opera House in New York City. Elizabeth, who walked with a cane as the result of injuries suffered in a fall, still showed her old sparkle and vitality as she came to the front of the stage. A roar of applause greeted her. For half a century she had been accustomed to criticism; such an outpouring of tribute and praise almost overwhelmed her.

Because she was unable to be on her feet for a very long period, Elizabeth had asked a friend to read her speech for her. This was probably the last time, she thought, that she would address such a large audience. She attacked two major themes. First, woman's duties must correspond to her capacity as an individual, not to her incidental role as wife, mother, sister, or daughter. Next, woman must have complete equality within the church.

Elizabeth was loved and admired widely, even though her ideas did not win popular acceptance. The public, like those who knew her well, responded to her intelligence and wit, to her courage and determination. Even ideas and deeds considered shocking and inappropriate in others were tolerated from this gracious elderly lady.

However, Elizabeth Cady Stanton's attack on inequality within the church provoked a violent storm when Volume I of *The Woman's Bible* was published later that month, in November 1895. Since the beginning of her work on the document in 1886, she had planned to force women to question their religious convictions. Her announced goal was to comment only on those passages which referred to women or obviously excluded them. She had hoped to ask Greek and Hebrew scholars to comment on the original texts and Biblical scholars to place the passages in history. She had written to many women, requesting help with the project. While many expressed interest and a few offered to help, most replied that it was wrong to tamper in any way with the Bible. Undaunted, Elizabeth decided, if necessary, to do all the work herself.

Especially disturbing to her was Susan's failure to support the idea. Her friend had been reared in a liberal Quaker tradition, which was more open to women than any other. She had not shared Elizabeth's struggles to free herself from the fears and repression of narrow dogma.

It was Clara Bewick Colby who became Elizabeth's staunch supporter in writing *The Woman's Bible*. Like Elizabeth, she was convinced that women would never achieve equality until they freed themselves from religion and the church. Clara Colby published some of Elizabeth's commentaries in her *Woman's Tribune* and editorially encouraged other women to help. Lillie Devereux Blake, the Reverend Phebe A. Hanaford, Louisa Southworth, and Ellen Battelle Dietrich, younger women activists who shared Elizabeth's religious perspective, wrote commentaries for the first volume, but the great majority of the work was done by Elizabeth Cady Stanton. Each woman cut out all the passages referring to women and pasted them in a blank notebook. Underneath she wrote comments.

Elizabeth was the author of the introduction. "From the inauguration of the movement for woman's emancipation," she stated, "the Bible has been used to hold her in the 'divinely ordained sphere' prescribed in the Old and New Testaments." She cited the Biblical teachings that woman had brought sin and death into the world and was condemned to bondage in marriage and suffering in maternity. Woman was commanded to depend on her husband for all her wants. Then she answered various criticisms that had already risen about *The Woman's Bible*. To Elizabeth Cady Stanton, the

Bible was no more and no less than the history and legends of a people as they searched for God.[85]

Her commentary on Genesis 1:27-28 (quoted above on page 107) was typical of her attempt to relate this search for God to women. "The first step in the elevation of woman to her true position," she wrote,

> as an equal factor in human progress, is the cultivation of the religious sentiment in regard to her dignity and equality, the recognition ... of an ideal Heavenly Mother, to whom their prayers should be addressed, as well as to a Father.

The concept of a Heavenly Mother she had first gained from Theodore Parker and William Henry Channing. She herself had often used it when she was asked to say grace at the table.

"If the language has any meaning," she continued,

> we have in these texts a plain declaration of the existence of the feminine element in the Godhead, equal in power and glory with the masculine. The Heavenly Mother and Father! "God created man in his *own image, male and female*." Thus Scripture, as well as science and philosophy, declares the eternity and equality of sex.[86]

To people who had been taught that the Bible was the direct and divinely inspired word of God, *The Woman's Bible* was heresy. Most of the reviews indicated strong opposition to the ideas Elizabeth and her co-commentators presented. But within a year, Volume I had gone through three American and two English editions. Among the few newspapers supporting Elizabeth were the New York *Sun* and the Chicago *Post*. Many clergymen preached sermons against *The Woman's Bible*. One of those who approved of it—the Reverend

Alexander Kent of Washington, D.C.—recognized it as not an attack on religion but an attack on false religious teachings about women. But many critics simply refused to see *The Woman's Bible* for what it was.

At the National American Woman Suffrage Association convention, in January 1896, *The Woman's Bible* caused a vigorous debate. Elizabeth had published the book as an individual, but her position as honorary president of the group and her long relationship with the association caused many to feel that she had damaged the entire movement. Rachel Foster Avery introduced a resolution declaring, "This association is non-sectarian, being composed of persons of all shades of religious opinion, and has no official connection with the so-called 'Woman's Bible' or any other theological publication."[87] Alice Stone Blackwell, daughter of Lucy Stone and Henry Blackwell; Carrie Chapman Catt, future president of the organization; and Anna Howard Shaw, minister, lecturer, and protégé of Susan B. Anthony, were among the younger members who supported the resolution. They did not want anything to divert attention from their central goal—to secure for women the right to vote. Lillie Devereux Blake and Clara Bewick Colby, who contributed to *The Woman's Bible*, were naturally opposed to the resolution. They were joined by such open-minded younger women as Charlotte Perkins Stetson (later Gilman), the "intellectual" of the second generation of feminists, and Mary Bentley Thomas.

As the debate intensified, Susan could not contain herself any longer. Leaving the chair, she came to the defense of her friend. Always, she insisted, the association has allowed each member the right to her own opinions.

131

The religious persecution of the ages has been carried on under what was claimed to be the command of God. I distrust those people who know so well what God wants them to do, because I notice it always coincides with their own desires.

She recalled that some had wanted to banish Ernestine Rose from their platform forty years ago because she had had unorthodox religious beliefs. "If Mrs. Stanton . . . had written *your* views," she accused,

you would not have considered a resolution necessary. . . . When our platform becomes too narrow for people of all creeds and of no creeds, I myself can not stand upon it.

She reminded the delegates that Elizabeth Cady Stanton had been criticized in 1848 for demanding suffrage for women, and in 1860 for favoring liberal divorce laws. In each instance, public opinion later became more accepting of her point of view. "If we do not inspire in women a broad and catholic spirit," Susan concluded her eloquent plea,

they will fail, when enfranchised, to constitute the power for better government which we have always claimed for them. . . . I pray you vote for religious liberty, without censorship or inquisition. This resolution adopted will be a vote of censure upon a woman who is without a peer in intellectual and statesmanlike ability; one who has stood for half a century the acknowledged leader of progressive thought and demand in regard to all matters pertaining to the absolute freedom of women.[88]

In spite of Susan's plea, the resolution passed. Elizabeth, who considered loyalty among the highest of virtues, was deeply hurt that her friend did not resign the presidency in protest. Never one to yield in her convictions, she nonetheless considered Susan disloyal to continue her association with the organization. But the friendship of half a century survived this difference of opinion as it had survived others. The younger and more conservative women urged Susan to listen less frequently to Elizabeth Cady Stanton and to concentrate solely on gaining suffrage. The liberals criticized Susan for focusing on only one of woman's problems and tried to persuade Elizabeth to condemn her.

Yet all efforts to divide the two women failed. Elizabeth knew that Susan's executive ability was necessary to organize the effort to secure the vote, even as she realized that having the right to cast a ballot would not remove all the inequalities so deeply entrenched in American society. Each used her talents in the way she felt would contribute most to woman's progress.

Elizabeth was hard at work on Volume II of *The Woman's Bible* amid all the controversy about Volume I. The first had covered only the Pentateuch; the second was to deal with the rest of the Old Testament and the New Testament, from Joshua to Revelations. It was published in 1898. Clara B. Neyman, Louisa Southworth, Lucinda B. Chandler, Phebe A. Hanaford, Matilda Joslyn Gage, Frances Ellen Burr, and Ellen Battelle Dietrich, who all shared Elizabeth's convictions about religion and the Scriptures, provided some of the commentary; again, most of the work was Elizabeth's.

Elizabeth was neither surprised nor discouraged by much of the adverse reaction. She was pleased to see that so many people were reading and discussing *The Woman's Bible*. Had she only caused women to think, she had won half the battle.

Also in 1898, Elizabeth Cady Stanton published her

autobiography, *Eighty Years and More*, a witty and lively account of her private life to complement her public record in the *History of Woman Suffrage*. It was as widely praised as *The Woman's Bible* was condemned. She was now a nationwide legend, admired and respected as the elder stateswoman of the women's movement.

Elizabeth was writing constantly. She sent addresses to the annual National American Woman Suffrage Association conventions and to congressional hearings even after she stopped attending them in 1892. In an article in *The Wheelman*, she assured women that they certainly should ride bicycles if they so desired. She continued to press for liberal divorce laws, cleaner cities, and, in all phases of life, more freedom for women.

As always, she took an active interest in politics and public affairs. She denounced the Chinese exclusion (Geary) bill in 1894. "How my blood boils over these persecutions of the Africans, the Jews, the Indians, and the Chinese," she commented. "I suppose the Japanese will come next. I wonder if these fanatical Christians think that Christ died for these peoples, or confined his self-sacrifice to Saxons, French, Germans, Italians?"[89] She sympathized with Eugene Debs and the workers during the Pullman Strike of 1894, and supported the Populists in their efforts to better the conditions of the common man.

To her great dismay, Elizabeth found that her eyesight was failing. She had to hire people to read to her, or enjoy the company of friends and guests who read aloud to her books they themselves wanted to read. "Oh, what a privation!" she confided to her diary.

I say nothing to my children of this great grief, but it is a sore

134

trial, with prospective total blindness! I will then be able to do nothing but think. However, I can still write without spectacles, though I can not read my own writing. But my hearing is as good as ever, and I am perfectly well otherwise.[90]

Among the books she had read to her were Andrew D. White's *A History of the Warfare of Science with Theology*, Boswell's *Life of Johnson*, Matthew Arnold's *Essays in Criticism*, Herbert Spencer's *Education*, Irving's *Oliver Goldsmith*, and novels by Charlotte Brontë, William Thackeray, and George Eliot.

Susan urged her to go to Washington for the 1898 celebration of the fiftieth anniversary of the Seneca Falls convention. "I am really getting too old for such things," she pleaded. But she sent two speeches, one ("The Significance of the Ballot") for the congressional hearings. Clara Bewick Colby read her message to the convention, "Our Defeats and Our Triumphs." Addressing herself to the theme, "Whatever affects woman's freedom, growth and development affords legitimate subject for discussion here," Elizabeth urged the younger women, in particular, not to limit the scope of their work.

Let this generation pay its debt to the past by continuing this great work until the last vestige of woman's subjection shall be erased from our creeds and codes and constitutions.[91]

Asked by Susan to draft a list of what she felt the association should do for its meeting scheduled for 1900, Elizabeth wrote that she favored a new government for Hawaii ("It is a disgrace to the civilization of the nineteenth century to make that island a male oligarchy."); she advocated a protest against the North Western Railroad for firing women from their jobs; she wanted a resolution passed against the Knights of Labor proposition to remove women from all jobs which take them out of the home ("Woman's work can never be properly organized in the isolated home."); she appealed for a broader platform that would include protests against all forms of injustice toward women; and she recommended holding the national convention in Washington, D.C., each year to pressure Congress more effectively.[92] That 1900 convention was the last at which Susan B. Anthony presided. After it she turned the reins of the organization over to Carrie Chapman Catt.

In her message to the 1901 suffrage convention, Elizabeth again entreated women to work as vigorously for equality within the church as they had within the state. Her 1902 message, read by the Reverend Olympia Brown, was on "Educated Suffrage." "The popular objection to woman suffrage," she contended,

> is that it would "double the ignorant vote." The patent answer to this is, abolish the ignorant vote. . . . There have been various restrictions in the past for men. We are willing to abide by the same for women, provided the insurmountable qualification of sex be forever removed.

Elizabeth considered it as important for a citizen to be able to read and write the English language as to be of age. "The growth of the mind should mean as much in citizenship as the growth of the body; perhaps even more."[93] She continued to resent the fact that not even well-qualified women could vote while all men who had just become American citizens, who were almost illiterate, could.

In May of 1902, Susan arrived to spend a week. Even

though they differed over the importance of the religious question, they enjoyed each other's company as much as ever. Then one day in June Susan paid another visit. She realized that, although Elizabeth was mentally as alert as ever, her physical condition was declining. As she prepared to leave, she said, with tears in her eyes, "Shall I see you again?"

"Oh, yes," Elizabeth answered cheerfully, "if not here, then in the hereafter, if there is one, and if there isn't we shall never know it."[94]

That October Elizabeth's children gathered in New York, realizing that she had not much longer to live. On October 12 her long article on the divorce question was published in the New York *American*. Elizabeth confided to her diary that she was deeply touched to receive a post card from an unknown woman in Chicago:

Today's *American* has a half-page that should be framed, or, better still, writ large or megaphoned everywhere. How many hearts today will thrill in response and how many heads will begin to think. It is by a Grand Old Woman. God bless her![95]

That was the last Elizabeth wrote in her diary.

Her keen mind active to the last, on October 25 she wrote a letter to President Theodore Roosevelt, urging him to bring about the "complete emancipation of thirty-six million women."[96] The next afternoon, sitting quietly in her chair, she died.

Susan B. Anthony was at home in her study when she received Harriot's telegram: "Mother passed away at three o'clock."[97] She sat there, beneath Elizabeth's portrait, until it grew dark. That evening a reporter came to interview her. Susan smiled sadly as she talked.

For fifty years there has been an unbroken friendship between us. We did not agree on every point, but on the central point of woman suffrage we always agreed, and that was the pivotal question. We never listened to stories of each other, never believed any tales of disloyalty of one to the other. Mrs. Stanton was a most courageous woman, a leader of thought and action. I have always called her the statesman of our movement. . . .

"What period of your lives did you enjoy the most?" inquired the reporter.

Quickly Susan replied,

The days when the struggle was the hardest and the fight the thickest; when the whole world was against us and we had to stand the closer to each other; when I would go to her home and help with the children and the housekeeping through the day and then we would sit up far into the night preparing our ammunition and getting ready to move on the enemy. The years since the rewards began to come have brought no enjoyment like that.

They talked awhile longer. Then Susan was once more overcome. "I can not express myself at all as I feel," she said.

I am too crushed to speak. If I had died first she would have found beautiful phrases to describe our friendship, but I can not put it into words. She always said she wanted to outlive me so that she could give her tribute to the world.[98]

Susan went to New York for the funeral. Only family and a few close friends were present to hear the Reverend Antoinette Brown Blackwell pay tribute to her beloved Elizabeth Cady Stanton.

At Woodlawn Cemetery, the Reverend Phebe A.

Hanaford committed the body of her dear friend to the earth.

In the following weeks, most American magazines paid tribute to Elizabeth Cady Stanton. Nearly every newspaper honored her memory with an editorial. The National American Woman Suffrage Association offered a memorial service at the annual convention in 1903. But it was Susan B. Anthony who summoned the eloquence which could only have come from a half century of friendship and partnership,

> As a speaker and a writer she was unsurpassed.... She combined in herself a marvelous trinity—reformer, philosopher, statesman. Had she been of the orthodox sex she would have been United States Senator or Chief Justice of the Supreme Court, but, belonging to the alleged inferior half of the human family, she died without having her opinions weighed in either the political or judicial scales of the Government.[99]

On August 26, 1920, American women finally achieved the right to vote. No one could overestimate the debt they owed to the woman who, in 1848, had first suggested in public that they deserved that right. She refused to limit her efforts to working for suffrage. Many of the other rights for which Elizabeth Cady Stanton fought are still denied to her countrywomen. But her spirit, her courage, and her eloquence continue to inspire those who carry on the struggle.

FOOTNOTES

1. Elizabeth Cady Stanton and others, eds., 6 vols., *History of Woman Suffrage* (New York: Fowler & Wells, 1881-1922), 1:70-71.

2. *Ibid.*, p. 72.

3. Elizabeth Cady Stanton, *Eighty Years and More* (New York: European Publishing Company, 1898), p. 4. Unless indicated otherwise, this autobiography is primary source material for this work.

4. Most of the dialogue in this biography is quoted from conversation or based on narrative in *Eighty Years and More.* Some bits of discussion and speeches are taken from the *History of Woman Suffrage*; these and other quotations from Stanton's letters and diary are footnoted throughout. Not more than ten sentences of dialogue are "made up," and in those instances, I tried to follow what I feel would have been said.

5. The following incident is related by Alma Lutz in *Created Equal* (New York: The John Day Company, 1940), pp. 16-17.

6. Theodore Stanton and Harriot Stanton Blatch, eds., 2 vols., *Elizabeth Cady Stanton as Revealed in her Letters, Diary and Reminiscences* (New York: Harper and Brothers, 1922), 2:4-5.

7. Birney polled 30,000 votes in the 1840 election.

8. Union between England and Ireland.

9. Lutz, p. 35.

10. *ECS*, 2:16. Letter of May 1, 1847.

11. *History of Woman Suffrage*, 1:63-74 for complete account of this convention.

12. Eleanor Flexner, *Century of Struggle* (New York: Atheneum Publishers, 1970), p. 75.

13. *ECS*, 2:19. Letter of September 14, 1848.

14. *Ibid.*, p. 21. Letter of September 30, 1848.

15. *Ibid.*, p. 26. Letter of February 11, 1851.

16. *Ibid.*, pp. 26-27. Letter of February 13, 1851.

17. *Ibid.*, p. 27. Letter of April 11, 1851.

18. *Ibid.*, pp. 35-36. Letter of October 14, 1851.

19. *Ibid.*, pp. 41-42. Letter of April 2, 1852.

20. *History of Woman Suffrage*, 1:481-83.

21. *Ibid.*, pp. 850-51.

22. *ECS*, 2:44-45. Letter of October 22, 1852.

23. *Ibid.*, pp. 55-56. Letter of January 20, 1854.

24. *History of Woman Suffrage*, 1:595-605.

25. *ECS*, 2:48-49. Letter of March 1, 1853.

26. *History of Woman Suffrage*, 1:860.

27. *ECS*, 2:82. Letter of June 14, 1860.

28. *Ibid.*, pp. 59-60. Letter of September 10, 1855.

29. It is unfortunate that so little has been written about Henry B. Stanton, a remarkable man whose career seems overshadowed by the accomplishments of his wife. It was not customary in the nineteenth century for wives to discuss or write about their relationships with their husbands, even in diaries. Elizabeth Cady Stanton revealed far more about her children, her friends, and even her housekeeper than she did about her husband. Further research might answer some of these questions.

30. *ECS*, 2:60.

31. Gerrit Smith was one of several abolitionists who contributed financially to John Brown's raid on the arsenal at Harper's Ferry, Virginia. To the abolitionists, Brown was a hero even though most Americans thought him at best insane.

32. *History of Woman Suffrage*, 1:708.

33. *History of Woman Suffrage*, 2:200.

34. *ECS*, 2:90-91. Letter of September 11, 1862. Horace Greeley and many of the abolitionist leaders, along with several more radical politicians, concluded that Lincoln could not win reelection in 1864 and should be replaced. During the summer of that year, when the war was not going especially well for the Union and when Lincoln was opposing radical plans for reconstruction in the South after the war, Greeley and his friends proposed another Republican convention to replace candidates Lincoln and Andrew Johnson, a Tennessee Democrat. After the fall of Atlanta and the beginning of Sherman's march to the sea in September, news from the battlefront became more encouraging. Lincoln defeated General George McClellan, the Democratic candidate, by a narrow popular margin.

35. *Ibid.*, p. 90. Letter of September 11, 1892, to Elizabeth Smith Miller.

36. *Ibid.*, pp. 94-95. Letter of July 20, 1863, to Nancy Smith.

37. The Stantons wanted Fremont to receive the Republican nomination because they believed he would end slavery immediately. (The Emancipation Proclamation of 1863 had freed slaves in rebel states only. There were still slaves in Maryland, Kentucky, Missouri, and other Union states.) The Stantons and their fellow abolitionists believed that ending slavery was more important than preserving the Union. Lincoln, on the other hand, wanted to end slavery in such a manner as to preserve the Union.

38. *ECS*, 2:355.

39. *Ibid.*, pp. 104-5. Letter of May 25, 1865.

40. *Ibid.*, p. 106. Letter of April 5, 1866.

41. *Ibid.*

42. *History of Woman Suffrage*, 2:225.

43. *Ibid.*, p. 270.

44. *Ibid.*, p. 284.

45. *Ibid.*, p. 285.

46. *Ibid.*, pp. 116-17, 287.

47. *Ibid.*, p. 119.

48. *ECS*, 2:119-20. Letter of January 8, 1868.

49. Northern opponents of the Civil War.

50. *History of Woman Suffrage*, 2:317.

51. *Ibid.*, pp. 333-34.

52. Foster was not criticizing Elizabeth and Susan for ridiculing blacks; rather he was condemning their association with Train, a known racial bigot. *The Revolution*'s official stand for educated suffrage was in fact in direct conflict with the universal suffrage officially advocated by the Association. Elizabeth and Susan strongly objected to giving the right to vote to *men* who could not read or write English before granting suffrage to women of *any* level of learning. They believed that too many uninformed and uneducated immigrants were being "bought" by the political "bosses" rather than voting from knowledge and conviction.

53. *History of Woman Suffrage*, 2:381-83.

54. *ECS*, 2:126. Letter of May 30, 1870.

55. Harriot Stanton Blatch and Alma Lutz, *Challenging Years: The Memoirs of Harriot Stanton Blatch* (New York: G.P. Putnam's Sons, 1940), pp. 4-5.

56. *History of Woman Suffrage*, 3:27-28.

57. See Stanton Blatch and Lutz, pp. 248-49; also Alma Lutz, *Susan B. Anthony* (Boston: Beacon Press, 1959), p. 321.

58. *ECS*, 2:153-54; Letter of January 14, 1878.

59. *Ibid.*, p. 171; Letter of August 2, 1880.

60. *Ibid.*, p. 177.

61. *Ibid.*, p. 178.

62. The suffrage movement itself was never forgotten while the *History* was going forward. The two women held a series of conventions in New England during the spring of 1881. Elizabeth

continued some speaking engagements and other writing.

63. *ECS*, 2:210.

64. *Ibid.*, p. 226.

65. "Eliza Eddy's husband had taken their two young daughters away from her and moved to Europe with them. She suffered greatly, and her father, Francis Jackson, gave much money to the women's cause. She herself left $56,000 to be divided between Susan and Lucy Stone." Lutz, *Susan B. Anthony* footnote, p. 313.

66. Elizabeth Cady Stanton, "Has Christianity Benefited Woman?" *North American Review*, 140 (May 1885), 390-99.

67. Elizabeth Cady Stanton, "The Need of Liberal Divorce Laws," *North American Review*, 139 (September 1884), p. 242.

68. *History of Woman Suffrage*, 4:58.

69. *Ibid.*, p. 59.

70. *Ibid.*, p. 60.

71. Quoted by Lutz, *Created Equal*, p. 264.

72. *ECS*, 2:236.

73. *Ibid.*, p. 237.

74. *Ibid.*, p. 242.

75. *Ibid.*, p. 251.

76. *Ibid.*, p. 252.

77. *History of Woman Suffrage*, 4:165-66.

78. *ECS*, 2:260-61.

79. *Ibid.*, p. 261.

80. *Ibid.*, p. 265.

81. *Ibid.*, p. 274.

82. *History of Woman Suffrage*, 4:189-90.

83. *ECS*, 2:282.

84. *Ibid.*, p. 285.

85. *The Woman's Bible*, 2 vols. (New York: European Publishing Co., 1895-98), 1:7.

86. *Ibid.*, pp. 14-15.

87. *History of Woman Suffrage*, 4:263.

88. *Ibid.*, p. 264.

89. *ECS*, 2:294.

90. *Ibid.*, p. 325.

91. *History of Woman Suffrage*, 4:292.

92. *ECS*, 2:345-46.

93. *History of Woman Suffrage*, 5:32; *ECS*, 2:364.

94. Ida Husted Harper, 3 vols., *The Life and Work of Susan B. Anthony* (Indianapolis: The Hollenbeck Press, 1908), 3:1256.

95. *ECS*, 2:367-68.

96. *Ibid.*, p. 369.

97. *Harper*, p. 1262-63.

98. *Ibid.*

99. *Ibid.*, p. 1263.

BIBLIOGRAPHY

Flexner, Eleanor. *Century of Struggle*. New York: Atheneum Publishers, 1970. The extensive bibliography will refer the reader to books about many of the persons with whom Elizabeth Cady Stanton worked during her long involvement in the woman's rights movement.

Lutz, Alma. *Created Equal*. New York: The John Day Company, 1940.

——. *Susan B. Anthony*. Boston: Beacon Press, 1959.

Stanton, Elizabeth Cady. *Eighty Years and More*. New York: European Publishing Company, 1898.

——. *The Woman's Bible*, 2 vols. New York: European Publishing Company, 1895-1898.

——. Susan B. Anthony, and Matilda J. Gage, eds. *History of Woman Suffrage*, 3 vols.; Susan B. Anthony and Ida Husted Harper, eds., 3 vols. New York: Fowler & Wells, 1881-1922.

Stanton, Theodore and Harriot Stanton Blatch, eds. *Elizabeth Cady Stanton as Revealed in Her Letters, Diary and Reminiscences*, 2 vols. New York: Harper and Brothers, 1922. The first volume is an annotated version of *Eighty Years and More*; the second volume contains selected letters and diary entries.

About the Author

Mary Ann B. Oakley is a first year student at the University of Washington Law School. A North Carolinian, she received her B.A. from Duke University and her M.A. from Emory University, where she began research on Elizabeth Cady Stanton. She and her husband, a pediatrician-epidemiologist, have three children.

Feminist Press Books for Adults

In order to rediscover and recreate the history and achievements of women, The Feminist Press will publish a series of biographies and reprints. Presently our priorities for pamphlets include American women of the nineteenth and twentieth centuries, women involved in working class struggles, women in the civil rights and black liberation movements, women in minority groups, women in science, law and other professions.

Feminist Press Biographies ($1.50)

Elizabeth Barrett Browning by Mary Jane Lupton. The life of the nineteenth century British poet who wrote the feminist verse-novel *Aurora Leigh*.

Elizabeth Cady Stanton by Mary Ann B. Oakley. The life of the first American woman to demand in public (in 1848) that women be allowed to vote.

Feminist Press Reprints ($1.50)

The Yellow Wallpaper by Charlotte Perkins Gilman. A neglected masterpiece by one of America's major feminist writers who explores a woman's descent into insanity. With an afterword by Elaine R. Hedges.

Life in the Iron Mills by Rebecca Harding Davis. A powerful short story about the lives of American working people, first published in 1861. With an afterword by Tillie Olsen.

Feminist Press Books for Children

In an effort to change the character of Children's literature, The Feminist Press will publish books about the lives of girls today and about women in history; books about one-parent families and about families in which both parents work and share household responsibilities. We are also looking for stories written by children about their experiences, feelings, thoughts.

Children's books now available:

The Dragon and the Doctor by Barbara Danish. A fantasy for young children, $1.00.

Challenge to Become a Doctor: The Story of Elizabeth Blackwell by Leah Heyn, with illustrations by Greta Handschuh. A biography for older children, $1.50.

THE FEMINIST PRESS ORDER FORM

	Price	Quan.	Amt.
Elizabeth Barrett Browning	$1.50		
Elizabeth Cady Stanton	$1.50		
The Dragon and the Doctor	$1.00		
Challenge to Become a Doctor	$1.50		
The Yellow Wallpaper	$1.50		
Life in the Iron Mills	$1.50		

POSTAGE AND HANDLING

$.25 for first book, $.05 for each additional
book up to ten. We will pay postage for
pre-paid orders of ten or more.
Please add local sales tax where applicable.

ENCLOSED PAYMENT

Subscription* $25.00 _____

Contribution $ _____

Send check or money order to:

The Feminist Press
10920 Battersea Lane
Columbia, Maryland   21043

*This entitles you to all Feminist Press publications in 1972 as
well as the two children's books currently available. Some of this
money will help to support the continuing work of the press.

SOLD TO:	SHIP TO:
Name	Name
Address	Address
City	City
State Zip	State Zip